BOUNCING BACK FROM THE EDGE

PHYLLIS JEMMOTT

Copyright © 2024 Phyllis Jemmott All rights reserved.

No part of this publication may be produced, distributed, or transmitted in any form or by any means, including photocopying, recording, or other electronic or mechanical methods, without the prior written permision of the publisher, except in the case of brief quotations embodied in critical reviews and certain other noncommercial uses permitted by copyright law.

For permission requests, write to the publisher, addressed "Attention: Permissions Coordinator" at the email address below:
Life and Success Media Ltd
e-mail: info@abookinsideyou.com
www.abookinsideyou.com

Unless otherwise stated, all scriptural references are taken from the King James Version of the Bible. Other versions cited are NIV, NKJV, AMP and KJV. Quotations marked NIV are taken from the HOLY BIBLE, NEW INTERNATIONAL VERSION. Copyright © 1973, 1978, 1984 by International Bible Society. Used by permission of Hodder and Stoughton Ltd, a member of the Hodder Headline Plc Group. All rights reserved.
"NIV" is a registered trademark of International Bible Society. UK trademark number 1448790. Quotations marked KJV are from the Holy Bible, King James Version.

BOUNCING BACK FROM THE EDGE
ISBN: 978-1-7384586-1-5
Cover Design: **MIA**Design.com

CONTENTS

PREFACE [7]

INTRODUCTION: Fatherly Instructions [11]
CHAPTER 1: Father And Son Relationship [19]
CHAPTER 2: Give Me My Portion [29]
CHAPTER 3: Father And Son Relationship [39]
CHAPTER 4: State of Want [47]
CHAPTER 5: Raymond's Confession [65]
CHAPTER 6: Enough is Enough [77]
CHAPTER 7: Crossing Gates [87]
CHAPTER 8: Confronting Fear [111]
CHAPTER 9: Facing Health Issues [119]
CHAPTER 10: Bounce To Freedom [131]
CHAPTER 11: Home Sweet Home [145]
CHAPTER 12: Living in Harmony [159]
CHAPTER 13: Abundant Living [175]
CHAPTER 14: Spiritual Sustenance [189]
CHAPTER 15: Sharing your Story [211]
CHAPTER 16: Celebrating a Come Back [229]
CHAPTER 17: Re-Adjusting After The Edge [245]
CHAPTER 18: Church Attendance [261]
CHAPTER 19: Abiding on the Straight and Narrow [279]

DEDICATION

I dedicate this book to all my Grand-sons,
Ryan, Marlon, Stephan, Reece, Devotee and Shiloh;

The contents of this book can be utilised as a tool-kit for your lives as you journey through the unknown.

With much love and affections.

PREFACE

Many people may have ignored the golden opportunity envisioning and reflecting on the possibility of improving life through various privileges that were offered to them after bouncing back from the edge. Some may have postponed the offer in hopes that opportunities will knock on their door once more. Unfortunately, sometimes opportunities only knocks once. Then, it's gone. A second chance might be possible if you remain in a positive, expectant and anticipatory readiness.

The awareness of the possibilities of the un-expected, whatever might happen through opportunism, may unfortunately become dim through carelessness, disobedience, or rebellious behaviors. Nevertheless through a hopeful outlook, a second chance to seize an opportunity may arise. Though you may not be fully granted exactly what you desire, or have lost, acknowledging the need for turning and repenting, will eventually draw you into a better state, where you will anticipate bouncing back from the edge to freedom from the past.

You may have questioned such ambition as: 'What about the time and other resources I have squandered making a mess of my life?' Or, you may have fallen so low that you wonder whether restoration from such a deliberating state to anything worthwhile, is possible. No man or woman is personally worthwhile to serve the Lord on their own terms. They will need intervention from above to cause an attitude adjustment to create a right spirit to equip that man or woman for service.

For instance, when an individual is captured by the spirit of pride, ambition, selfishness, envy, lovelessness and a critical spirit, or any number of these bad attitudes, the result is defilement of the whole personality. Even when an individual feels disconnected through circumstance, being cut off from family, no longer participating in a life affirming Christian community, there is still hope if he will try again to turn his life around. He will eventually experience a renewal, if he seeks restoration and remains in Jesus. While there is life there is hope of 'what's left!'

You must understand that you are valued and chosen with a new identity as a child of God. Many other examples regarding people bouncing back from the edge are included in this book. God saw you when other people gave up on you. He saw you wandering on the banks of the edge. If and when you put one foot in front of the other, endeavoring to bounce back from the edge of despair, He will see that what He could make out of you is priceless!

He saw the real person in you and has plans for your life: for you to teach others through your experiences. He saw that you are capable of loving others who have been rejected, thrown out, demoralized and hated. He saw you as a person of compassion, an encourager, and helper to the poor. He saw you telling the story 'come see a man that took me up and put me back together' as you share the story of receiving salvation: love, hope and expectation,

Jesus saw you, standing at the edge of your extremities wondering which way to turn: left or right, going forward, or going backward, life or death. Yes, He was there and would not let you make the wrong choice because you had not yet fulfilled your earthly assignment: to tell the world about His love and how He rescued you from the edge of destruction. He implored you to choose life! Though you were not worthy of the precious gift of life, Jesus reached out His hands in love and compassion. Somehow for a brief moment you saw a ray of hope and held on tightly and bounce back from the edge to regain positivity to live victorious.

Lord my father, you uphold all who have fallen and though they fall they are not utterly cast down. Those who are bowed down by oppression and affliction You are able to raise up. You are ready to answer the prayers of Your people. Thus my mouth shall speak Your praises.

Lord, You are gracious and full of compassion to those who serve You. The people who have tasted Your unfailing love shall talk of Your goodness to them who fear You.

INTRODUCTION
FATHERLY INSTRUCTIONS

It is with great enthusiasm and pleasure I introduce this incredible story of a life changing book. This book presents Bouncing Back from the Edge which is a follow up from a previous work: 'The Edge.'

This rendition contains relevant stories and illustrations for every nationality, age, gender: rich, or poor there is a chapter to pique your interest. Inside each you will experience useful information, questions and some answers for many of the circumstances that life may throw at you.

Bouncing back from what you have lost, borrowed, rob of or having been charged unlawfully, unfairly and unreasonably. Bouncing back from the residual effects of the behaviors of persons whom you've always trusted, to say the least, there is more for you to take from this book.

This book is written about a father and his two sons: Raymond the younger and Ronald the elder. Both sons had their own personalities. The father loved both equally. The younger son is highlighted in this story as a jolly, carefree and spirited young man. While growing up, among other boys in his community, he attended secular school; and regular Sunday school with his brother accompanied by his father.

Raymond acted more confident and mature than his older brother; and behaved far more vigorously than his age. He was not afraid of taking chances, even if he knew he may suffer the consequence later on down the road. His brother Ronald was more reserved and cautious in decision-making style; a thinker a *'stay-at-home'* and obedient son. Nevertheless, Ronald would speak out whenever he thought Raymond's behavior towards their father was unreasonable.

For example, Raymond asked for his portion of inheritance from his father at an early age and went out and wasted it. This is what young people often do: seeking a way out that looks good and easy but not counting the cost. Having no experience with handling sudden riches was his down fall. He should have waited at home under his father's jurisdiction for many more years where he would have learned the realities of life, such as money management.

Introduction

He took his case and away he went into a deep hole from whence he could never find his way out. At the very end of his spending spree he returned home penniless and embarrassed. Yet, even before Raymond asked forgiveness, his father's heart was touched with feelings of compassion for his son, as he saw him approaching from a distance. So he called for the best robe, the newest shoes, a ring of sonship, and the fattest cow restoring him to his rightful place in the family. The fattest cow was prepared in celebration of his return.

There are some useful examples of a father's instruction as love letters to his sons. 'My beloved sons, '… give close attention to the Word of God, Why? The Word and acknowledgement of wisdom will enable you to make decisions that will leads to salvation. The Words of God are the fountain and standard of wisdom and understanding. Many wise things may be found in human compositions but divine revelations are wisdom upon which you can build.

The father reiterated, another important point: you must be in prayer; cry after knowledge; lift up the voice for understanding because heaven is whence this good and perfect gift comes. Therefore, speak for it, vote for it, and submit your tongue to the command for wisdom.

Be willing to take pains, as seeking for silver; preferring it far over the wealth of the world. Labor in search as those who dig in the mines and consider what success will come from these endeavors.

He instructed his sons regarding their endeavours that they will not be in vain if they follow certain principles. 'You will understand the fear of the Lord, that is, you will know how to worship Him aright. You will also know how to conduct yourselves towards all men. You will understand by the word of God: righteousness and judgment, equity, the principles of justice, charity, and fear dealings which will make you fit for every relation and faithful to every truth.

He strongly emphasized all grounds with examples of how God bestowed and imparted wisdom. Not only giving newness and understanding but causing man to understand that God is not stingy gives what is best. He is not only wise but is wisdom, Himself. He has blessed the world with a revelation of His will. He speaks out of His mouth the law to the prophets through the written words by His ministers. Then comes knowledge and understanding. Thus, a full discovery of truth and goodness will make you knowledgeable and intelligent.

Introduction

The father reminded his sons that God has promised particular plans to good men who are sincerely disposed to do His will. You shall have that knowledge and that understanding if you are obedient. Therefore, if you depend on God and seek His wisdom, to uphold you, He will enable you to keep the path of judgment, for He preserves the way of the saints, in order for you to work out your salvation for God who works in you. Thus, true wisdom will keep you from the path of sin, and will do you great kindness and enrich you with the wealth of the world.

He strongly endorses the power of wisdom, *'When wisdom has the entire possession of you, it will keep you. When it enters your heart as the leaven into the dough it is likely to do you good. Moreover, wisdom will preserve you from corrupt principles, atheistically profane men, who make it their business to debauch young men's judgment, and instill into their minds prejudices against religion.'*

The father expounded how wisdom will deliver you from the ways of evil men; their walk and tendency to persuade you to walk in their way towards evil desires. They seemly leave the righteous way, in which they were trained to walk, for the way of utter darkness that hates the light, where men appear to be led blindfold by ignorance and error.

The wise father warns his sons against some women whose ways are crocked as a great many windings and turnings to escape the pursuit of their convictions.

A great error to be avoided is the evil behavior of certain women who take pleasure in sin. Both in committing and seeing others doing the same; rejoicing in opportunities to do evil. For instance, women of corrupt practices will lead you to fleshy lust, which defiles the body, these are called strange women which you ought to shun. She speaks fair, and tells how much you are admired above any man, flatters with her words, which has no true affection for you or any concern for your welfare any more than Delilah for Samson. She has in mind to pick your pocket and gratify a base lust for her own, thus, taking heed to the sin of whoredom. It is a sin that has a direct intent of the killing of tthe soul; as the extinguishing of all good affections and dispositions. Beware! Discretion will preserve every man, not only from evil woman, but from the evil house, the house that inclines to death. He urged, 'Wisdom will keep you from all familiarity with the worshippers of images known as false gods. There is only one God, Jehovah is His name!

The wise father continues to inspire his sons in the knowledge of wisdom's ability to keep them from being captivated by the carnal mind and from subjecting the spirit to the dominion of the flesh. This wisdom is useful to guide and direct you into that which is good that you may walk in the way of good men. It will be wise of you to walk in that way, to ask for the good old way, and by studying the path of the righteous is the path of life. The father gave encouragement to his sons: imitate excellent persons such as the patriarchs and prophets of old. They were preserved as righteous men who followed after right examples and never got distracted from the ways of wisdom. In comparison to the people of the world who cannot understand those things because they haven't been given to them, but to you it has been given, a blessed privilege to know your father's love.

As the familiar phrase, 'Like father, like son' implies that children grow into becoming like their parents. But here, God warns His people not to be like their fore-fathers, who disobeyed Him and reaped the consequences. You are responsible before God for your actions. You are not trapped by your heredity or environment.' Don't use these excuses for getting away with wrong doings. You ought to learn the lessons of your father so you will not repeat the mistakes of others.

Follow in a father and son relationship!

Chapter 1

FATHER AND SON RELATIONSHIP

A father is a motivator, helper, coach, friend, and provider for his family. It is an honorable role, as every child cherishes loving, fatherly instruction, discipline, and encouragement. Fathers serve as disciplinarians, employing a stern yet caring approach to teach, train, and guide their children with wisdom.

The responsibilities of a father are vast and often challenging, especially during a child's formative years. This period of growth can be a testing time for both parents and children. It requires abundant patience, understanding, and a steadfast commitment from fathers to raise their children in the fear and knowledge of the Lord.

Raising children in a Godly manner can be especially challenging for fathers, as it requires immense love, patience, and dedication. However, clear guidance is provided in God's Word, which serves as a reliable road map. Fathers are encouraged to seek wisdom diligently, and when they find it, to use it in training their children in the way they should go so that, when they are older, they will not depart from it.

It is equally important to teach children the value of honoring their parents. Scripture commands children to honor their father and mother in the Lord so that their days may be long. This includes obeying parental instructions—whether from Christian or non-Christian parents—so long as these instructions align with God's will.

A child's duty is to show respect, esteem, admiration, and honor to their father. However, fathers must also take care not to provoke their children to anger. This can happen through actions such as losing their temper, undue severity, favoritism, cruelty, suppression, or misuse of authority. Instead, fathers should strive to provide a nurturing environment filled with fairness and understanding.

Fathers would do well to seek positive examples and practical methods to guide their children safely, steering them away from visible and hidden dangers. The lasting impact of a father's words and actions cannot be overstated:

many children carry their father's teachings into adulthood, using them as a foundation when raising their own children.

THE SIGNIFICANCE OF HONORING YOUR FATHER

To honor your father means more than mere outward obedience: it requires inward respect and reverence. True honor stems from the heart, aligning with the great commandment that comes with a promise: honoring and obeying parents ensures a long and prosperous life on earth.

A STORY OF A FATHER'S RELATIONSHIP WITH HIS SONS

There is a story about a father and his two sons, Ronald and Raymond. Ronald, the older son, was a homebody who never challenged his father. Raymond, the younger son, was restless and eager to experience life outside the confines of his father's home.

One day, Raymond decided to leave. He hurried into a far country, confident in his ability to navigate life independently. Craving the excitement of the world, he sought freedom from his father's authority, determined to taste everything the world had to offer—both good and bad.

However, Raymond soon discovered that life outside his father's house was not as glamorous as he had imagined. His choices left him in despair, feeling like a failure and consumed with regret. Facing unbearable circumstances, he decided to return home, humbled and longing for reconciliation.

Raymond's journey is a timeless lesson about the consequences of disobedience and the redemptive power of returning to a place of love and safety. His story, told even today, reminds others to consider their choices carefully and seek God's guidance in all things.

THE FATHER'S BLESSING

The concept of a father's blessing holds profound importance throughout Scripture. As Abraham believed in the power of a father's blessing, he spoke over his son, saying, *"My son is like the smell of a field that the Lord has blessed"* (Genesis 27:27).

Isaac, too, embraced this sacred practice. When he blessed his son Jacob, he expressed affection and approval, saying, "See, the smell of my son is as the smell of a field that the Lord has blessed" (Genesis 27:27). In Old Testament times, a father's blessing was a cherished institution. It consisted of two key elements:

A MEANINGFUL TOUCH

A father's blessing often included the laying on of hands, a kiss, or an embrace. These physical gestures symbolized acceptance, love, and the transmission of divine favor.

SPOKEN WORDS OF AFFIRMATION

Affirming and affectionate words from a father to his child conveyed approval and encouragement. Such blessings were acts of faith, not mere sentiment or favoritism.

When Isaac blessed his children, he acted on God's behalf, using his divinely delegated authority to impart blessings. This practice reflected God's truth and demonstrated the father's vital role in shaping his children's lives.

THE CALL TO BLESS

Every child longs for their father's blessing, and every father is called to bless their children. Just as Isaac blessed his sons, fathers today are encouraged to speak life, love, and encouragement into their children's lives. The father's blessing is a powerful, enduring legacy—a gift that nurtures and strengthens both the child and the family.

A father is generally proud when the firstborn is a boy. Boys are expected to carry on the father's name from one generation to another. However, all children are blessed by God, the giver of each person's life. Thus, fathers should never allow negative words spoken towards their sons or daughters to be demeaning or insensitive. Instead, fathers should use affirming words such as, *"I am proud to call you my son,"* even when their sons or daughters are not making the right choices.

Unfortunately, some fathers may be absent from the family home, and others, even while present, may not have the tendency to hold tightly to the reins of control to keep children from making mistakes that could otherwise be avoided. Nevertheless, a father's obligation and goal are to take the initiative to allow independence gradually as children grow to maturity and are able to manage their own responsibilities.

It is wise and important for fathers and their sons to establish a good relationship, with the expectation that their sons may one day become fathers themselves. Previously, in the introduction, a father had two sons—

Raymond, the younger, and Ronald, the elder. Both sons had different characters. Ronald was reserved and austere, sober with good humor to those in his company, adhered to his education, and was not easily distracted.

The younger son, Raymond, was impatient, greedy, and selfish. He asked his father for his inheritance, to which the father agreed, even though he correctly assumed, *"My son will waste his money."* Raymond spent all his inheritance and became penniless, friendless, homeless, and destitute.

The father reached out in prayer for his lost son day and night—prayers that bore an effectual reward for his son's deliverance. Somewhere down the road and through life, prayer carved a path that led Raymond back home to his Father. Prayer shone a bright light to guide his weary steps amidst the dark path of pride, greed, and rebellion. Raymond realized it would be a privilege if he could adopt some of these prayer points of his father in the coming days, as he planned his journey back home.

Although Raymond was in a state of carrying dirt and a foul smell, needing a haircut, with nails grown long like a hawk and in desperate need of fresh grooming, he had never been sick unto death. He often reflected, *"It must have been the prayers of my father that kept me wholesome. Though many times I've experienced heartbreak and pain, there was nothing seriously wrong with me physically. Mentally, I may need medical attention."*

Although his hopes seemed unreachable—far from bouncing back from the edge—he reasoned, *"If hope is activated, there might be a possibility of bouncing back from the edge to reach home."*

Raymond thought of several possibilities for how to move safely away from the edge, but he wondered how. He maintained his belief that there is always a way out of every dreadful situation: when prayers reach the throne room of God, the impossible will become possible. Raymond's next intention was to plan his actions at this critical point. He realized he could not move forward with guilt hanging over him any longer. He had to act now or perish—and he was not content to perish. Instead, he decided to confess to God, his Creator, and also to his father.

He thought carefully about what to say in his confession. He confessed with his mouth and believed in his heart. His confession was heard by both God and his father. It was done—the great transaction was complete. Confession is the answer for a heart that needs to be cleansed of wrongdoing, call it what it is—sin. The blood of Jesus washes away sin and cleanses us from all atrocities of the flesh, bringing freedom in Jesus' name.

In the following chapter, it is evident that this was the kind of confession Raymond made. He sought forgiveness and confessed by acknowledging the specific sin of which he was guilty. In capital letters and bold writing, he wrote: REBELLION AGAINST MY FATHER'S AUTHORITY.

RAYMOND'S PRAYER

....

Father I come to you in my sad state of body, soul, and spirit. I am sorry for the things that I have done to myself and to my loving father, please forgive me.

I acknowledged my sins and they are ever before me, please forgive me, and prayed earnestly,

'Father in heaven, my name is Raymond and I come to tell you sorry for what I've done to you and my father. 'I confess that I was wrong and promise never to engage in such sins ever again, please forgive me, in your name Amen.

BOUNCING BACK FROM THE EDGE

Chapter 2

GIVE ME MY PORTION

It was a sad and disappointing day when Raymond, the father's youngest son, requested his portion of the inheritance due to him. He said, *"I will never expect anything more."* In other words, he presumed that would be it—whether he wasted or spent his portion, it would be his responsibility. *"Father, give me my share, my ownership. I want my piece of the inheritance. I want my own family."*

Raymond and his father had a good relationship, and there was no indication of any conflict between them. It wasn't as though Raymond and his father were at odds; otherwise, the father would have discerned the tension and provided guidance to address the issue before it escalated.

They were not in a business partnership where profits were legally shared or divided. There was no arrangement entitling Raymond to a portion of the estate based on contributions or labor over the years. With that in mind, consider the following questions if you were in the father's situation:

• Did Raymond sign a legal document with his father, witnessed by others, granting him the right to ask for his portion?

• Did he work as a shareholder to improve the business and make it more productive?

• Was there an agreed timeline to divide the increase? If so, when, and what was the expected amount?

In contrast, Raymond's older brother had not made any such request. He was more mature and likely understood family principles. He knew that, according to Old Testament teachings, a father was not obligated to hand over his inheritance to his children until after his death. Nonetheless, some parents may choose to distribute their legacy before their passing. However, this choice comes with risks: parents may outlive their children, leaving nothing for themselves in their later years.

One day, Raymond decided to leave his father's house. That morning, he was up earlier than usual because he had

Give Me My Portion

been unable to sleep soundly the night before. All night, he wrestled with the bright idea of leaving home to explore the wide world. He had preconceived plans but chose not to disclose them to his father or brother. Instead, Raymond kept his plans tightly locked away, revealing nothing until he had walked out the door of his father's house.

The morning arrived bright, with blue skies and not a drop of rain to dim his plans. Raymond had already received his portion of the inheritance, which he tucked away in multiple hidden compartments, out of sight from his father and, perhaps, his mourning brother. The father did not question Raymond about how he planned to manage his affairs or where he intended to live. He resisted the temptation to ask too much but still inquired, *"Raymond, my son,"* he said, *"have you thought about working hard to make a living, perhaps getting married someday and having children or grandchildren?"*

Raymond could not answer these questions. His mind was elsewhere, and he remained silent, not in the mood to talk. He packed his belongings into bags, slung them over his shoulder, and walked out the door. He did not ask for prayers of journeying mercies; instead, an anxious compulsion drove him hastily away from his father's protection.

Raymond was heading into a wide, cruel, and dangerous world. He had no idea how greed and selfishness would become his greatest downfalls in a crowded, diverse world filled with people of all nationalities, cultures, and ages. It would be a lonely place for someone like him.

Raymond had just closed the door to fellowship, love, and care from a loving father. No sooner had he stepped through that door than he found himself entering a world that seemed to spiral toward destruction. At first, he felt the cold breeze of the harsh world blowing against his face. It resonated deep within him, whispering, *"Go ahead and get ready to explore."* Here, at last, was freedom—freedom from a locked-up mentality, free to do as he pleased, whenever he pleased, without restrictions. Spoiled by the idea of doing whatever he wanted, he quickly dismissed the reality of his actions and moved forward with his plans.

Raymond had no idea what awaited him in this wide, wicked world—an unfriendly environment filled with people from different races, cultures, and backgrounds. He had never imagined such a place, nor could he have known that his money would not last without others demanding a piece of it. He quickly learned that in this world, there were those who would take advantage of his generosity, or worse, manipulate him. Though he was raised in the comfort of his father's home and had never been accustomed to the harshness of the outside world, he was soon forced to adopt behaviors that went against everything he once knew. Drinking for hours, indulging with women, and rough sleeping became part of his new reality.

At first, Raymond was excited by the worldly pleasures. He never complained, joining in as long as his money lasted. His thoughts never turned to the balance of his finances; he lived in the moment. With the insidious looseness surrounding him, his so-called friends wore his clothes without asking permission, never bothering to clean them, only tossing them aside as soon as they were done. Slowly, he developed a conscience that had no voice—a deadened sense of right and wrong. He leaned heavily on booze to get through his days, and from start to finish, his life became one of reckless abandon.

Raymond had been warned about the dangers of indulging with women of loose morals, but he ignored the advice. Like many young people, he shut his ears to the truth, blinding himself to the consequences of his actions. The intoxicating wines of intellectualism, materialism, and deception—along with the dulling of his conscience—fed his persistent disobedience. Raymond trusted in his financial means rather than turning to God, the true source of his well-being. In his ignorance, he traded away his righteousness for fleeting pleasures, for aesthetic, social, and moral reasons that lacked any objective reality. It was as if he were in a deep sleep, unaware of the damage being done.

When Raymond finally realized how quickly his funds had been depleting, it was too late. He had been so caught up in wasting and spending, never taking the time to check his balance. There was no robbery or any bad people demanding his money. He hadn't even considered helping anyone in need. He often passed by rough sleepers on his path, but he never spared a glance or felt pity. He was too busy enjoying the bright lights and pleasures of the day. He never imagined that one day he would find himself as desperate as those he had ignored.

Before leaving his father's house, Raymond had been confident in the misbelief that he was missing out on the pleasures of the outside world. He had no idea he would experience such emotional turmoil. He missed the authority of his father who used to tell him what to do and how to accomplish it, as well as the big, annoying eyes of his elder brother. Unfortunately, Raymond had forgotten the principles his father had taught him. He hadn't taken the time to seriously consider even one line of his father's advice on the pleasures of life because he was so caught up in his busy, carefree existence. He was living in the moment, laughing, and doing whatever made him happy on the outside.

But then, suddenly, memories from his past started to resurface. He couldn't shake them off. He remembered family devotion times with his father and his older brother. It was his turn to read the Bible, and the scripture taken that day read, *"Remember your Creator in the days of your youth, before the days of trouble come, and the years approach when you will say, 'I find no pleasure in them.'"*

He suddenly realized, with a pang of guilt, "It's me, Raymond," but in his congested mind, he quickly dismissed the thought and closed his ears to the truth. He felt like a blind man stumbling through the darkness, lacking the guiding light of wisdom. It was a dreadfully isolated place, and he was terrified. He thought back to the edge of the path he had once been carried from, and cried out, "Help me! Will somebody help me?" But there was no one there to guide him away from the danger. It was a pitiful condition. Raymond had run out of money and was now living on his own, without direction, vulnerable to the dangers around him.

He had been warned about the dangers of venturing out into the world, but he had ignored all the advice, choosing instead to close his ears. As the saying goes, *"He who cannot hear will feel."* Like many young people desperate to leave their parents' authority and explore the unknown, Raymond had no idea what his fate would be. Sadly, when the unexpected happens, it is often the parents who are left to pick up the pieces from their children's mistakes. Some children, in their disobedience, even end up returning in a casket to be buried under the cold clay. Every parent knows that children aren't always easy to teach. People have their own wills and must choose whether or not to follow the instructions of their parents and leaders. Discipline is part of the process, and every child should understand the consequences of disobedience, but in the end, the choice is theirs.

For Raymond, the choice had to be made. He thought of his father though he did nothing about returning home. The road he was on was not smooth, and it only got worse. Eventually, he would have to face an unpleasant end if he continued down this path. He knew he had to make a move, leave the edge of danger, and return to his father's house.

Now broke and desperate for work, Raymond didn't want to become a beggar. One day, he saw a sign that read: *"Work Available: Feeding Pigs."*

PIG FEEDER APPLY WITHIN

....

Raymond quickly seized the opportunity and applied for the job of feeding and tending to pigs. Though it was far from the job he had envisioned for himself, especially considering that, according to his religion, pigs were considered unclean animals, he was desperate for food and lodging. He was willing to accept the job just to earn a living. He had no prior experience working outside his father's farm but beggars have no choice but to adapt to their circumstances.

Raymond accepted the job, even though the pay was meager. He was forced to eat whatever the pigs left behind, finding himself in a degrading condition far worse than anything he had ever imagined. It felt like a fate worse than living on the edge of poverty. Yet, despite his despair, he still held on to a faint hope for a better tomorrow—a hope that one day, he would return to his father's house.

As he reflected on his situation, Raymond realized that he had no one to blame but himself. *"Fancy me, Raymond, accepting the worst job there is,"* he thought to himself. *"When I consider it all, I can only blame myself and no one else."*

Chapter

CONSEQUENCES OF CHOICES

Wrong choices can lead to serious consequences that may affect an individual's future life significantly. For instance, making hasty decisions about important matters—whether right or wrong—can result in outcomes that are often regrettable and have long-lasting impacts on one's life and position. Correct choices are often applauded, but wrong ones can bring about considerable consequences.

Everyone, regardless of status—rich or poor, great or small—is susceptible to making mistakes. As long as humans are involved, errors are inevitable, and some may come with severe consequences.

At times, people may stubbornly declare, *"I don't care what anyone says; I'm going to do it anyway."* Such a statement clearly indicates a closed mind, unwilling to consider advice. Even when advice is sought, it may only be heeded if it aligns with the decision already made; often because it represents an easier path. It is human nature to resist help and insist on doing things their own way.

Some individuals fail to consider the consequences of their actions until it is too late. When character is lost, hasty choices often follow—choices that can haunt a person for a long time, leaving them constantly reflecting on the experience. The wisest course of action is to seek advice from trusted individuals before making final decisions.

Often, the state of your mind during decision-making is unclear to you. In such moments, the enemy of your soul may whisper distractions: *"Don't delay—go ahead and sign that document; it's your only chance."* However, it's crucial to pause, seek professional advice, and dispel your fears, particularly when dealing with important matters like legal documents.

At times, hidden fears may cloud your confidence, obstructing the clarity offered by God's word, which is designed to guide your choices. This is when you must stop and listen for the inner voice of warning and support. Temptations—such as the allure of prohibited pleasures over virtuous paths or dishonesty over integrity—may press upon you. However, trusting God for wisdom and strength offers a path to make better choices and avoid regrets.

Take, for example, the story of Raymond. Once a young man of good character, he made choices that led him astray, costing him dearly. He felt unworthy to be called his father's son and believed his identity had been reduced from a position of honor to one of shame.

Raymond's mistakes stripped him of his father's protection, confidence, and even his sense of self-worth. He lost his brother's friendship and the comforts of home—family devotions, laughter, warm meals, and security. Despite his failures, Raymond's inner voice urged him to reflect on his past and take action. Though he doubted his right to reclaim his place in the family, he realized the importance of seeking restoration.

The story highlights the powerful lessons of making wrong choices and resisting the urge to surrender to despair. Life's adversities may bring sorrow and offense when others try to offer solutions, but it's important to remember: while you may have created the mess, there is always hope for change if you stop, reflect, and persevere. Never give up, because as long as there is life, there is hope.

Every choice has consequences. Wrong decisions often carry a hefty price. For instance, parking in a prohibited zone—even briefly—may result in a ticket. Returning to your car to find a fine, you'll regret the decision, especially if funds are tight. Yet, the fine must be paid—there's no excuse. Ignoring it could lead to court appearances or even the loss of your license.

Life's lessons teach us that choices matter. By pausing to reflect, seeking guidance, and trusting in God, we can navigate challenges and avoid costly mistakes.

If you choose to walk in the middle of the road instead of using the level crossing, you're taking a deliberate risk—not a mistake—that could result in dire consequences, such as being hit by a passing vehicle. Consider this: what if the driver is not qualified, is under the influence, or becomes distracted by a fleeting thought? They may not even notice you standing or crossing the road. Always think of the potential consequences before making such a choice.

Many individuals, young and old, find themselves behind bars today because they took unnecessary risks—chances that could have been avoided had they paused to think before acting. When the sentence for those choices is handed down, feelings of regret, anger, or despair can overwhelm them. Yet, at that point, what's done is final.

This is why it's essential to think carefully before acting. Hasty behavior, bad attitudes, and overconfidence—*"playing too big for your boots"*—are common causes of poor decisions. Don't allow minor disputes or mistakes to escalate into significant problems. Instead, be humble and apologize early if necessary to prevent issues from spiraling out of control.

Peer pressure can also lead to disastrous outcomes. Don't let it dictate your choices. When the prison doors slam shut, you'll be left alone to reflect, without the comfort of your parents' protection or advice. You'll be on your own to face the consequences. So, make wise decisions, and don't let small, impulsive actions rob you of your freedom and future.

Take the time to read the fine print, whether in contracts, agreements, or rules. Never dismiss even the smallest detail, as it may hold significant importance. Be wise—don't blindly follow the crowd. Instead, develop your own judgment and make your own decisions.

Avoid bad company, as not everyone has your best interests at heart. Be selective about who you surround yourself with, and steer clear of those who encourage shortcuts, like making "quick bucks." These paths rarely end well.

Instead, focus on building a meaningful life. Pursue education, enroll in college, and work diligently to achieve your goals. Strive to become the best version of yourself, even if some people call you a coward for not taking unnecessary risks. Finding your own identity and owning it is far more valuable than trying to fit into someone else's mold.

Remember, the choices you make today will shape your future. Choose wisely, think deeply, and walk the path that leads to success and fulfillment.

PRAYER

....

Father God, I never had an earthly father to guide and protect and be an example that I could follow and emulate. Please adopt me as your son, and I promise with your help

I will do my best to live for you for the rest of my young life. Let me know you have answered this prayer. I thank for that you are available that I can talk to you each day, whether I'm glad or sad. In your name I ask. Amen.

BOUNCING BACK FROM THE EDGE

Chapter 4

A STATE OF WANTING

The future is like an uncharted sea of the unknown, holding both joys and terrors, comfort and pain, love and loneliness. Some people live in fear of what tomorrow might bring, wondering what evils lurk in the shadows. Others turn to fortune-tellers, seers, or future-telling practices in a desperate attempt to uncover the secrets of what lies ahead. However, the truth remains: tomorrow is known only to God and the special messengers to whom He has chosen to reveal future events.

In every society, across all ages and cultures, the pervasive spirit of rebellion is evident—from the royal palace to the humblest dwelling. No one is exempt from its influence. The most dangerous form of rebellion, however, is that which is directed against our Creator. Since ancient times, humanity has been quick to blame God for their troubles, often setting themselves in opposition to His divine wisdom and governance over the human race.

History has shown that humans are incapable of truly governing themselves. No matter how advanced our systems of rule or how noble our intentions, humanity's attempts at self-governance inevitably fall short. Without divine guidance, individuals struggle to care for themselves and their neighbors adequately. It is in surrendering to God's will and acknowledging His sovereignty that true order, peace, and purpose can be found.

A REBELLIOUS KING

A well-known story is told of a king who developed a rebellious attitude toward God. Despite being granted the privilege of ruling over a great nation for many years, he failed to understand his role as a mere mortal under God's sovereign authority. He was warned repeatedly, even through vivid dreams that foretold his downfall if he persisted in disobedience. Yet, he ignored these warnings, continuing in rebellion until his pride and hardened heart became his master.

The king lived extravagantly, surrounded by servants who bowed before him and proclaimed, *"O King, live forever!"* Yet, he failed to consider that the Most High God, who reigns over the universe, sees all and governs over kings and nations alike. No one who rises against His authority can stand in His presence. The last rebellion of such magnitude occurred with Lucifer, who was cast out of heaven along with his followers.

Although the king had achieved great success, managing vast numbers of people from various nationalities and cultures, he foolishly viewed himself as lord over those who had no voice. However, nothing is hidden from the eyes of Almighty God. The king secretly harbored a desire to be like God—a task far beyond his reach. How foolish for a mere man, created from dust, to think he could rival his Creator, who made heaven, earth, and everything in them.

Yet, despite the king's arrogance, God remained merciful, kind, and longsuffering. He understands humanity's frailty, sinfulness, and inability to save itself. Such prideful thoughts should have never entered the king's mind. A ruler entrusted with the care of so many should have humbly acknowledged the supreme authority of the One who appointed him.

One night, the king had a dream that deeply troubled him. He sought an interpreter to reveal the meaning of the dream. When the interpreter was brought before the king, he listened attentively to the dream, though he was visibly shaken by its implications. The interpreter himself was astonished and hesitant, worried about how to deliver such a grave message to the king.

After much deliberation, the interpreter revealed the meaning of the dream. Despite the king's unease and his initial prejudice toward the interpreter—thinking about the interpreter's origins, nationality, and background—the interpreter forgave him and fulfilled his duty.

This act of forgiveness highlights a profound truth: many people in the world cling to unforgiveness and even take pleasure in the misfortunes of others. Yet, the interpreter rose above such sentiments, demonstrating grace and humility.

As he explained the dream, the interpreter described a great tree that grew large and strong, its top reaching the sky. The tree was visible to all, providing shelter for birds, wild beasts, and sustenance for many through its abundant fruits and branches. The interpreter then confessed his heartfelt wish that the dream's message had been meant

A State of Wanting

for someone else and not for the king himself, due to its ominous significance.

He said, your majesty, you have become a great and strong, *'Your greatness has grown until it reaches the sky, and your dominion extends to distance part of the earth'*.

The king often became upset when he received bad news, but the bearer of such news was not afraid to tell the truth, even if it was not what the king wanted to hear about his dream. The king was warned about his rebellious attitude toward God and urged to change his ways.

However, over time, the king did nothing. Despite being given ample opportunity to repent from his pride and rebellion—believing himself above both divine and royal law—he chose to live life on his own terms, stretching the boundaries of what was acceptable. Tragically, justice came swiftly and unexpectedly. He had no time to ask for mercy, as he had waited too long. This is a solemn reminder of how some stubborn sinners will cry out on the final day, after years of ignoring God's call to turn from their wicked ways: *"Mercy gone, judgment come."*

The king believed he had plenty of time to do as he pleased, dismissing any notion of accountability. His rebellion grew worse, driving him to the farthest extremes away from God's mercies. One day, he walked around his palace, boasting about his greatness and proclaiming how he alone had built his majestic residence by his own might for the glory of his name.

But as his final words of pride left his lips, a loud voice thundered from heaven, echoing across the palace grounds.

It was the loudest voice the king had ever heard, and it declared, *"Your royal authority has been taken from you. The kingdom has departed from you. You have been deprived of your honor, and your reason has been taken from you. In losing your sanity, you lose your dominion. They will drive you away from men; in the same hour, you will be driven from the people, and you will live in the wilderness. You will eat grass like an ox. Seven times will pass over you until you acknowledge that the Most High is sovereign over all the kingdoms on earth, and He gives them to anyone He pleases."* (See Daniel 4:32)

Suddenly he felt stark naked, his understanding and memory was gone, and all the faculty of rationale was broken, and went naked, like a brute beast, and ran wild into the woods, and made to eat grass as oxen. His character was changed dramatically and causes him to behave and acting as animals. His heart the seat of emotion was changed from men to a beast heart, and adopting the heart like a beast. Instantly the king countenance was changed dramatically, and had a serious effect on his behavior, the king's heart as the seat of his emotion was changed to beast heart, adopting the behavior as beast. He had no human touch of emotions, neither feeling, hurts, compassion for others.

The king was in isolation humbling himself among the wild beast of the field. He looked in amazement where he was at the present, but did not fully understand because his mind was deeply disturbed. In such deploring state of mind the king was not fit to be in the company of humans. Therefore, he had to dwell in the fields behaving as other animals. By then his hair grew long enough like the eagle feather, some would described it as natty dread. His finger nails had grown like birds claws, now days it was as extension, his toe nail on his feet grew in length, he was destined spending considerable time examining himself.

The king thought he was more than a man, but God made him less than a man and put him on a level with the beast that set up rival with his maker. During that time of despair and shock he considers his past luxury once enjoyed in the palace. He looked around in amazement in his present state. In such deploring state of mind he was only fit to be kept away from humans dwelling in the field where he could roam about like the other untamed animals with no human instincts.

In the king's pride, haughtiness and abuse of God's patience, as he walked in the palace in pomp and pride, he thought to himself: everything in his palace looks great! He had no idea the palace was built before he was born but he boast that he was the one who built it. As he boasted a powerful word came from heaven by which the king was immediately deprived of his honor as a king. He would be spared from these atrocities because God is patient, kind, long-suffering and does not take pleasure in bringing man down from their pomp and pride in a hurry.

His only hope was confessing his ignorant thinking and take positive actions to clear his head; to repent and ask big God, the Supreme Creator for His forgiveness. After years in this terrible state the king regained consciousness, he came to himself and humbled himself. He realized he was not the Creator of himself; but that he is mere flesh and blood apt to make mistake. Most importantely, there was a higher power that ruled over human beings that should be respected, obeyed.

You may be tempted to ask:, could this befall a man? Answer: surely it can! When men get besides themselves comparing themselves as God that will be the results. The moment the king owned up, made confession with his mouth believed in his heart, he was in recovery mode, The level of his testimony, the splendour was returned to his former state because he repented and confessed his sin. He was restored to prominence. He bounce back and sat on the throne it was greater than before. This is what happen when a person see themselves and don't like what they see, take action and become sorry and make a turn around, and repented.

THE KING IS RESTORED

On the basis of his testimony and the confession of his sin, the king was restored from distraction and thinking too highly of himself. Having regained his right mind, he said, *"I lifted up my eyes to heaven,"* and saw himself no longer looking as a beast, but looking up as a man, as a penitent, as a humble petitioner for mercy.

The use of his reasoning was restored to a right mind to glorified God, and become humble in an attitude from bad behaviors. It is a fact that men never righty use their reason till they begin to be righteous. Thus, his folly was the means whereby he became wise; to bring him to himself, whereas first he was beside. Because people have always flattered and complemented the king with words such as, O king live forever, but now he was convince that no king lived forever, but the God of Israel only.

When restoration is granted towards an individual, there was no interruption, the affliction would not last any longer than when the work for which it was sent, for the glory of God, and for the humbling of his pomp and pride. He was made to realize he is mere sinful man, and that God is Jehovah Majesty, Ruler, of the earth and heaven ruling sea and land, moon and stars. God's kingdom is like Himself, everlasting and His dominion from all generation to generation, all nations before Him are as nothing.

The king now has his kingdom restored to him, and is established in his kingdom as if nothing had been interrupted. His affection was no longer work than the time they were sent. *'How was the king resorted?*

After his restoration, he realized that God should be praised, extoled, and honoring the king of heaven. Eventually, the King regains consciousness and wondered where he was, and who he was, and actually realized he was just a piece of clay made from dust of the earth.

He became humbled and realized he was not the maker or Creator of his own self, there is a higher power that ruled over human beings, to be respected and obeyed. He realizes that man is but flesh and blood that is apt to make miserable mistakes and hasty decisions. You may wonder could this happen to a normal person? *'Yes it could,'* when men thought too highly of themselves and acting in desperation to become as the Creator of themselves, this is like treading deep waters, how on earth could this mere man wants to be a king like the King of Kings.

It was not until the end of the appointed time that he lifted up his eyes to heaven, and his understanding returned to him, and he praised God and honored him, and made confession and repented of his folly idea of fighting against his Creator. God is merciful and would rather not delight to cut off mankind in their ignorance but rather given time to see themselves and acknowledge God the true ruler of man and the universe.

However, the moment the king repented of his bad behavior and confessed his wrong doings, he was in line for recovery from his past state of shame, demotion, bought down to the lowest of the lowest made an example of rebellious people. It was the biggest showdown for someone with such pomp and pride, self-made authority among high society to be bought down so low and not in the state of human beings but rather behaving like animal.

It must have being devastating when he regained consciousness and came to himself. The show- down was not caused by the doings of another person's like himself, the king, no; it was by the hand of the Almighty God's justice and power. Although it might be difficult enduring hardship, yet, when a season of success comes your way, your behavior should change to disallow strange attitude going to the head, causing disruption of boastful attitude leading to a down fall.

For instance, before Lucifer was cast out of heaven he was not contented to be in God's presence. He wanted to be exalted above all other spiritual powers; to be placed above the clouds; above the Shekinah glory and most of all to be like the Most High God. The people who followed the pattern of their leader, believed as though they can become gods through thinking too highly of themselves. God would not, and will not tolerate any revilers, contenders, in His presence, He shall remain God of the Most High and men must be cast out, and learn mannerism, and repent and turn from their evil ways. Eventually the king's mind was restored; he was able to bounce back from the edge of rebellion.

REBELLIOUS BEHAVOUR OF AN ARMY GENERAL

....

A rebellious behavior can drastically developed in a person who refuses to conform with convention and rising up against authority. The spirit of rebellion is often the cause of disobedience against authorities. Interestingly, rebellion is a failing and hopeless disposition which will never succeed in winning a war, nevertheless winning a battle against God the Creator of heaven and earth, is not possible. It would be waste of human effort quarrelling with God. How could mere man be in such rebellious contest with Almighty God?

The story is told of an army general of a great army. He had potential on earth and a favorite of heaven, yet, he was struck with a disease, which without an intervention, would certainly be mortal. It is appointed to men that they will die and afterwards the judgment. This sickness in his body had seized him in the midst of his triumph over large armies, and he was not prepared for death and wish it will never come any closer.

In his tragic moments he was seriously and tragically defected because late in his life he became proud, and arrogance, and ceased to develop spiritually, and apparently lapsing into backsliding, turning away from God, and turning to evil. Many evil ideas enter his heart through the spirit of jealousy, pride, and arrogance without him taking stock of his rebellious behavior. In previous years the army general had turned away his heart from God. During that time he developed a haughty spirit of heart blindness; he became dissatisfied with his condition and started murmuring and lusting after material things that displease that it was God who caused his blessing to be withheld.

Instead of taking heed of the sin of his own heart sin he quickly passes the blame on to God. The Question is often asks, *'Is anyone afflicted with sickness?* Answer, *'Let him pray'* It is a powerful thought that prayer works as salve for every sore, or broken heart, whether personal, or to the public. Prayer does not bring God down to us, but brings us up to Him. It's a fact how affliction do create a desire to read the bible and also to bend your knees in prayer. Before this tragic illness got hold of the general he lost his confidence and became ashamed as a high profile. While he was in good health he often went up to the house of the Lord to pray.

It was good and profitable act of preparation for his healing from his illness. He did not delay reaching out in prayer before he became sick because some kind of sickness, he may have restrained his ability to pray, especially sickness of the mind. Some will pray 'Lord keep me in perfect peace and let my mind be stayed on you'

When the army general was sick in bed, he turned his face to the wall, perhaps looking death in the face saying, *'You, Mr. Death, you have no power over my body until God says so.'* He did not demand a reward from God to proclaim his rights, of being right in his heart, and hoping God exempt him from doing wrongs, and see his heart and healed him.

Though he believe the fervent prayer of a righteous avails much, and the effectual and that fervent prayer makes the difference, and when he was losing his grips, he came to himself and made confession to God. He cried and wept bitterly, *'Lord remembers how I have walked before you in truth and sincerity and with a perfect heart'* He became sorry for himself with questions such as, *'Why me?'*

The basis of self-pity is selfishness, similarly, to people who tend to been sorry for themselves, are seldom truly sorry for others. Their entire attention *'Me, me, and me'* If you find yourself at the edge of rebellious behavior and still maintaining a desire to bounce back to good health, immediately seize opportunity to pray, confess all known sins to God and believe Him for healing and deliverance. Thus, the basis nature of praying is talking to God, a basic principle of sincere Christian living. When you pray it is advisable to follow the model prayer in (Matthew 6).

The time came when the general turned away from his attendants and poured out his heart to God in brief and fervency prayer watering with tears and called God's attention to his blameless record. He remembered how to pray, so he did during his sickness. God had mercy and sent an answer by His Spirit to be of good cheer, assuring him his prayer is heard and his sins are forgiven, and whether he live or die will have no reason to believe that he prayed in vain, in case he was doubtful if his prayers were heard.

God gave the general repeated signs of assurance of His favor, though it had seems was too little. The sign was the going back of the shadow upon the sun dial, the sun a faithful measure of time, to gets the clock going can be set back, when He pleases, for the Father of all lights is the directory of them. The general was careful to give God thanks after his recovery. He wrote a memorial of his affection and the frame of his own heart when he was close to the edge of his existence and thought of himself as gone forever. Yet, God in his mercy brought him from the edge from his rebellious attitude. He was able to live victoriously until taken from this world.

REBELLIOUS BEHAVOUR OF AN ARMY GENERAL

Lord of heaven, had it not for you who have been on my side I would still be living among the wild beast of the field, but it is by your mercies that abides forever that spare us, 'O Lord my God, I earnestly plead for your help in times of trouble. Help me to number my days and to recognize that I'm but mere man, and you O Lord are Jehovah Amen.

Chapter 5

RAYMOND'S CONFESSION

Confession is described as a godly sorrow for sin, maintained by repentance, and resulting in salvation. When a person decides to confess, it is a good and positive action. Self-confession is a powerful source that promotes emotional health, brings release from inward dissatisfaction, and leads to a state of freedom—freedom from obligation, the unrestricted use of a right or privilege, and ultimately repentance.

While Raymond was growing up, he was somewhat reserved but maintained a reasonable relationship with his older brother and was surrounded by the love of his father. However, when he walked away from his father's house and traveled to a far country, he eventually came to his senses.

He realized the gravity of his mistakes and felt deep sorrow for his actions.

At a critical point in his life, Raymond recognized the necessity of confession. He acknowledged the miserable state he was in and understood that this was not about his brother or father—it was about himself alone. Raymond could not shift the blame onto anyone else; he had to take full responsibility for his actions.

Initially, when Raymond considered making a confession, it was a means of coming to terms with how he saw himself. He was desperately in need of relief and pardon for his wrong attitudes toward both God and his father. In that moment, Raymond found himself in a good place—one of self-awareness and humility—acknowledging that there was hope and help in asking for forgiveness.

When an individual decides to confess, it often stems from an inward discomfort, a sense of unease about having done wrong or strayed down the wrong path. Yet, despite the discomfort, making a confession is undoubtedly the right thing to do.

Raymond's affliction brought him to a place of genuine reflection and deep longing, causing him to come to his senses. When he realized that earthly possessions and pursuits could not make him truly happy, and after trying every other means to ease his suffering, he recognized the insufficiency of worldly solutions. At that pivotal moment—marked by the right timing, the right desire, and the right action—he chose to return home to his father.

In times when your heart and spirit are overwhelmed, it becomes essential to confess and wholeheartedly pour out your burdens before the Lord. Doing so reflects the freedom God gives us to approach Him openly and the liberty of speech we have in His presence. It also reveals the relief that comes to an afflicted spirit when humbly expressing its grief and grievances to Him.

Grief is deeply personal and cannot be easily compared or explained. Even those closest to you—family and friends—may not fully comprehend the depth of the pain and anguish you bear. Yet, prayer acts as a soothing balm for the soul. It penetrates the depths of suffering, ministering to the wounded areas and bringing renewal and restoration where there was once despair.

Self-confession is a personal act of owning up to one's wrongdoings, asking for forgiveness, and making sensible and positive choices to turn away from those actions. It is an essential step toward cleansing the mind and heart from flawed thinking. This is exactly what Raymond did—he acknowledged his mistakes, admitted he had done wrong, and made the decision to turn to God for help.

Raymond's confession was heartfelt and honest. He admitted his true condition and humbly said to his father, "I've sinned; I'm not worthy to be called your son." His repentance was genuine, demonstrating that the choice is clear: either repent or remain in a miserable state.

His confession was sincere: *"I have sinned. I've been rebellious towards my father's authority. I'm in a bad place and need help. I can't help myself. I must take the blame—no one else put me in this condition. I caused all this trouble myself. There's no one else to blame. Please forgive me."*

Raymond's humility and willingness to take full responsibility for his actions paved the way for his restoration.

Self-confession means agreeing with God about your sin. It involves more than just acknowledging the wrongdoing; it requires a sorrowful heart for the sin and a willingness to turn away from it. While it doesn't mean you will never commit the same sin again, it does indicate a genuine attitude of repentance. Raymond recognized this and acted on it. By following his confession with prayer and openly confessing his faults to his father, he found healing for his guilty conscience and was set free to move forward with the strength of forgiveness.

True confession is the only way to be liberated from past guilt. While you may choose to carry guilt, you don't have to. The moment you put your trust in Christ, He cancels the record of your past. You no longer have a past; you only have a future. Jesus took away your sins by nailing them to the cross. God promises to blot out your sins, ensuring that they will never be remembered again.

Everyone must confess their wrongdoings. Confession is required for pardon—acknowledging where we've gone wrong and seeking forgiveness. Confession is followed by repentance, vowing never to commit the same offense again. Sometimes, this process needs to be repeated daily, as we, as individuals, are often guilty of sinning against God and one another.

Some individuals may make a confession but break it just as quickly as they make it. However, this young man, Raymond, meant every word of his confession. It was intentional and deliberate. Confession of sins is crucial, and repentance and forgiveness must be part of an individual's life. Sometimes, people become ashamed of their sinful ways and, in their desire to give up evil habits, they risk unconsciously drifting away from Christ. It is essential to recognize that it is the power of Christ that draws us to Him, resulting in spiritual renewal, quickening, and an outward life transformed under the influence of the Holy Spirit. The goal is never to stray backward but to make the right choices in serving God.

In this way, Raymond's confession helped him reconcile with his father through obedience. When he compared his former state to his present condition, reflecting on where he had gone wrong and where he now found himself, he had a serious conversation with himself. He came to his senses and made the decision to return home. First, he became sorrowful for his wrongdoings. He turned away from his sin and repented. Although, after claiming his birthright, he understood that he would no longer have any further claim to his father's estate.

It is natural when people find it in their hearts that they confess their sins to God and also make confession to one another's for causing offence. It has a great effect on both individual to explain how they feel towards each other. The father had yet heard his son's confession and was willing to abide by the implications of it. Which is a mark of genuine repentance. Raymond prepared his mind and questions, *'How many hired servants my father and I'm suffering with hungry.'*

He considered how bad his condition was, and how better it would be if he returns home to his father. Raymond purposed in his heart what to say; consideration is the first step towards taking action. He considered deeply how bad his condition was, said, *'I perish with hunger'.*

Thus, the father's attitude toward his son was compassion. *'Mercy rewrote his name, have mercy on my son dear Lord, I give thanks for your mercy'*

The father hoped his oldest son would also show mercy to his younger brother, understanding that one day, he too would need mercy. He hoped the older son would put this understanding into action. The father knew that it was not enough to sit idly in his condition and do nothing. He thought to himself, *"I will arise and go to my father."* Even though he was in a far country, every step taken toward his father's house was worth it.

True repentance is about rising and returning. It is deliberate and intentional—knowing what to say when you arrive home. It may be a hundred steps, but with each one, you draw nearer to your destination.

As you walk with God, you will find terms like forgiveness and mercy especially useful on your journey.

FORGIVENESS

....

Forgiveness is a term used to describe the pardon of a fault or offense, or the excusal from payment of a debt owed. In the Old Testament, God is portrayed as both a forgiving God and one who holds people accountable for their guilt. He is the source of forgiveness which is provided through the sacrificial system.

When you receive forgiveness, it is akin to having a debt paid off. Imagine having to give up work to care for a loved one, and the debts start to pile up. As you struggle to find a job that pays enough to clear them, you can feel overwhelmed by the weight of your financial burden. But when God steps into the situation, it all changes. Suddenly, the debt is wiped out, and the relief is profound. You wonder why you carried that weight for so long when God was ready to take care of it all along.

This experience can be a powerful lesson in your walk with God—realizing how sin creates a wedge between you and God, but also understanding His love and forgiveness. You no longer need to carry the weight of sin on your own. It's a problem if you try to keep your feet in both worlds—wanting God's help while also holding on to things that make you feel good.

The burden of sin will be lifted. It will no longer be your problem. In return, you can enjoy God's forgiveness and serve Him with a grateful heart. As you grow in maturity, you'll learn that God allows you to make choices that shape your life—whether to step away from sin or to entertain it. Growing in grace and in the knowledge of truth is a continuous process. It requires acknowledging your flaws and weaknesses and addressing them by staying devoted to God and His purpose.

To become humble, you must approach God with humility, engaging in prayer and fasting, and making wise decisions. Prayer and fasting are powerful tools against the spirit of pride, while fasting is an assault on lust. Giving to

God's work is the greatest assault on the spirit of poverty and greed.

SELF-CONDEMNATION

....

Raymond's story illustrates the power of self-reflection and the weight of regret. As he refrains from blaming others, he takes full responsibility for his actions and reflects on the state of his life. Despite being a son of a wealthy father, living as a prince, Raymond realizes that his choices led him to a place of emptiness. This realization drives him to make a decision: to arise and return home.

"I have sinned" becomes the urgent declaration of his repentance. Despite his circumstances, Raymond retains enough integrity not to beg for mercy, but instead accepts the consequences of his actions with sincerity. His regret is deep, and he wishes that neither he nor anyone else had to face such a painful experience. It is often through sorrow and tragedy that people are brought to the point of seeking help from the only one who can truly heal and restore.

This reflection raises a question: Are you living your life in a way that disregards responsibility and commitment? Do you, like Raymond, acknowledge the need for change when your actions lead you astray? The road to healing begins with genuine self-awareness, and Raymond's journey serves as a reminder of the importance of repentance and the courage to return to what is right.

REBELLIOUS BEHAVIOUR OF AN ARMY GENERAL

Grace is undeserved acceptance and love received from another. While biblical terms for 'grace' are used in various ways, the most characteristic meaning refers to an undeserved favor granted by a superior to an inferior. When referring to divine grace toward mankind, it speaks of the undeserved favor of God in providing salvation to those deserving condemnation.

In a more specific Christian sense, grace refers to the saving activity of God, manifested in the gift of His Son, who died in place of sinners—or in Raymond's situation, a state of rebellion. Grace, therefore, is the source of salvation, faith, and justification. It embodies the great and manifold riches of God. As Ephesians 1:7 says, *"In Him we have redemption through His blood, the forgiveness of sins, according to the riches of His grace."*

Chapter 6

ENOUGH IS ENOUGH

In the past, Raymond had not valued his father's instructions or discipline, nor had he stopped to think before hitting rock bottom—a place that felt like being between a rock and a hard place. It was a place of self-discovery, filled with doom and gloom, yet he still held onto the hope that the best was yet to come. Therefore, after confession, action is required—repenting of all known sin and turning toward doing what is right.

Raymond came to a conclusion and remembered how many servants his father had hired while he was away, starving far from home. It became clear that returning home was the right decision, hoping that, perhaps, his father was still alive and would accept him back as his son. He first made a confession to himself: *"I will arise and go to my father."* This was a good thought, but it was only in taking action that the decision would truly matter. *"I will arise and go to my father."* That was the moment of action.

Though living in a distant country, a great distance from his father's house, Raymond resolved to take every step toward home. Despite his wounded heart, doubts, fears, discouragement, and the sight of the pigs grunting for the next husks, he was determined. The more he thought about his sad condition, the worse it seemed. He had no one to call—no father, brother, or friend to share his pain. He was truly alone.

At last, Raymond made a mental resolution: *"What should I do? How do I begin?"* He decided, *"Right, the next day, I will leave the pigpen and begin my journey home."* Though he had no idea how many miles lay between him and his father's house, nor how many days the journey might take, he was willing to face it. Perhaps it might take months to reach home, and by that time, his frail, weak body might not withstand the long, weary journey. But he knew he had to begin.

"I might not make it home to see my father," were some of the thoughts Raymond reflected on in his wayward mind. He decided to repent of his waywardness and began his journey back to his father, admitting, *"I've wasted every drop*

of my father's money on riotous living. Now I have nothing left—only misery, complaints, and regrets. Please help me."

Strangely, as he walked, his thoughts drifted to his eldest brother. *"Neither did my brother inquire about my whereabouts, nor did he come asking, 'Has anyone seen my little brother, Raymond?'"* However, he could hardly blame him. He had done things his way, and now he was paying the price. Raymond recognized that making a start, no matter how late, was a positive action. Yet, another distraction popped up: *"What will my master think when he comes looking for me, seeing the state of the pigs lamenting for their next meal after all these days?"*

Though his master had trusted him and would have no reason to suspect his unhappiness while feeding the pigs, Raymond wondered, "I've never made any formal complaints, never asked to be upgraded or requested a raise in salary. Yet, could my boss, using his instincts, see how I'm struggling with the pigs?" Nevertheless, Raymond resigned himself to his self-made life, telling himself, *"I've made my bed, and I must lie in it until some change comes."*

Raymond began his journey, and travelled all day and could hardly find his way, because of being so mixed up and pressured by what might hinder him from going forward. As night falls, hungry, weak and feeling alone and destitute, he took a break and lay by the side of the rough road. He could not give any account of where he was as he sat by the roadside lamenting what next. It was so late that evening no one passed by and night fall. He fell asleep and being so tired with foot pains he slept reasonable well but not soundly because of anxieties. Nevertheless he waited patiently for the morning to break. As the morning broke with blue skies, not a cloud of darkness, no breakfast to start the day, not even a hush of the pig's food, he said within himself, *'I can only imagine how sincerely my father is thinking and praying for me to find my way home'*

Raymond, the pig feeder, had had enough. He left the pigs behind and decided to run away from the edge of self-destruction, heading for his father's home before he destroyed himself completely. For three days, as he traveled, he took no notice of the people who passed by, who might have handed him a bit of bread or a drink. It was the same each day at different locations.

As he walked, Raymond began repeating a prayer his father had taught him and his brother. Sighing, he muttered, *"The Lord is my shepherd; I shall not want."* Though he was deeply and desperately in need now, he hoped that some good person would come his way and offer him a bit of help.

He anticipated that his father was at home, praying for his safe return, and that nothing could overrule the prayers of a loving father.

"My son is coming home," Raymond thought, silently praying, *"Our Father, who art in heaven, hallowed be Thy name. Give me this day my daily bread, and forgive me for what I have done to my father, and to You."*

This prayer brought Raymond some comfort. It gave him the strength to continue his lonely journey, taking each step with renewed determination. Though his father hadn't heard from him since the day he left home, and though Raymond hadn't kept in touch, they both lived far apart—out of sight, out of mind—but not on the father's watch. The father was always praying and hoping that one day his son would return home safely.

Suddenly, Raymond saw a small pond of water with a few sugar cane joints lying nearby. He quickly looked left and right, then reached out for a drink of water and a piece of cane, squeezing it to cool his thirst. Raymond thought, Prayer is useful. I must repeat this prayer more regularly. It has hope and provision built into it. Though I haven't been activating my belief, hope will keep me anticipating my future. It's not over until God says so.

Raymond was not far from his father's house, though he didn't realize the distance because his mind was consumed with thoughts of how his father would receive him back into the family home. His mind was filled with "What ifs," doubts, and second-guessing. But Raymond managed to separate these intruding thoughts and breathe deeply. *"God is able to see me through,"* he said to himself. *"He could have destroyed me already, but He chose to save me for His purpose. I will not die. I will live to see my father again."*

The last time Raymond traveled this road was when he left home, carrying money for travel expenses, and more to spend lavishly on his friends. What a difference, he thought. All my friends have moved on. They used and abused me to get me to part with my money. What a fool I was. I wasn't acquainted with the worldly life as they were. It seems I'm the only one left in this world, and I'm about to die from hunger. How true the saying is: *"Woeful wastes bring woeful wants!"*

Raymond left the pig farm without saying goodbye to the master or the pigs. He was escaping from the degrading atmosphere, dirty and smelling of pigs, while rehearsing his speech over and over in his mind—what he wanted to say to his father when he finally returned home. His speech was filled with sorrow and repentance, a reflection of his deep regret. He was seeking forgiveness not only from his father but also from heaven—from God Himself.

He had fully acknowledged that he had forfeited all the privileges of his family. He said, *"I am no longer worthy to be called your son."* In the most humble terms, he added, *"Make me one of your hired servants."* That would be good enough, perhaps even better than he deserved. If his father was willing to let him sit among the servants, it would be far better than living with the pigs.

Raymond took the right action, not avoiding his confession or trying to hide any part of it. He meant every word. It's interesting how, when someone is in the depths of desperation, they are often pushed to do the right thing, at the right time and place. It is possible to bounce back from a path of wrongdoing to one of righteousness. Yet, as Raymond reflected on how dirty and filthy he was from the pigsty, he continued onward, even though the very atmosphere around him was degrading for a son of a wealthy father.

While feeding the pigs, Raymond was saddened by the degrading nature of the work he was forced to do. Never in his young life had he been subjected to such a humiliating task. He thought to himself, "If these pigs were human, they might notice how my mouth is moving up and down as I talk to myself. Maybe they'd run away, thinking I was a madman." Even dumb animals can sense when something isn't quite right with their owners. A happy face often creates a happy atmosphere, but Raymond's face was far from joyful.

Despite this, there was still some inner courage left in Raymond, a spirit that resisted the weight of his despair. He managed to fight back the feeling of hopelessness with a positive mindset, whispering to himself, *"Hold on. Joy comes in the morning. Better days are ahead."*

Though nothing comes easiy, whether by chance or hard work, life requires you to put your shoulder to the wheel. Sometimes the wheel spins fast, and at other times it spins even faster. You must be ready to take immediate action when a change in direction is needed. The wheels of life turn round and round, eventually coming to a halt.

Still, Raymond kept his focus. He held on to the hope that better days were ahead, constantly reminding himself, *"I'm going home. Time is the master. During this waiting process, I must be prepared to endure the long haul, believing the result is already here, just waiting to be revealed at the break of day."*

PRAYER

....

Dear Lord, give me the courage to wait, in the meantime, and please renew my strength that I may not quit in the process of waiting on your timings. Consider and hear me, O Lord my God, enlighten mine eyes lest I sleep the sleep of death, lest my enemies say, I have prevailed against him, and those who trouble me rejoice when I am moved. Father God preserve me, O God, for in you, O Lord, do I put my trust, In Jesus name!

Blessed be the God of our Father Abraham, Isaac and Jacob, I've experience for myself the powerful manifestation of your favor and I'm grateful to you heaven Father. Lord I pray for wisdom, as I make decisions. I ask you to guard my thoughts and actions, and give me discernment to make wise choice.

I pray you will enable me to see the present situation from your prospective and make choices that are in your will for my life. Father God I trust in your wisdom and guidance for my life and pray that I would be open to hearing your voice at all times. May your mercies endure forever O Lord!

BOUNCING BACK FROM THE EDGE

Chapter 7

CROSSING GATES

A gate is similar to a door, wall, or threshold, as it sets a boundary between what is inside and what is outside. The term 'gate' is often more prominent, as it provides the most common access to towns, villages, temples, and even houses. In practice, a gate serves both to allow and limit access. An open gate permits entry, though gatekeepers are often employed to ensure that only authorized individuals gain access. A closed gate, on the other hand, offers protection and safety for those within. In this way, the gate of death marks the boundary between life and death.

Although Raymond had good intentions in returning to his father's house, he faced numerous challenges on the road to recovery. First, he had to confront and overcome several difficult gates, each presenting distractions and obstacles. If he could manage to cross over each gate, he would be rewarded. Raymond understood that he could not move forward on his journey of recovery unless he successfully navigated these gates.

On his journey, Raymond encountered several gates, one after another. These gates were not barriers to his destination but stepping stones to his divine purpose. He was not to be discouraged by the gates labeled despair, confession, repentance, forgiveness, discovery, and finally, the gate of acceptance. At each junction, he had to push through and break free.

You, too, are at a point where you must push and break through—demolishing every gate that stands between you and the life God has ordained for you.

GATE OF DESPAIR

....

The gate of despair represents a moment of hopelessness—a state of mind that leads one to consider dangerous and negative thoughts, perhaps even contemplating self-destruction. In such a place, a person may not realize how close they are to true danger, overwhelmed by feelings of inadequacy. This inner turmoil fuels two destructive enemies: doubt and fear.

These two forces work together, often inseparable. Where you find one, you will typically find the other, and despair adds its strength, pushing the vulnerable even further toward the edge. In this state, one may lose the will to seek help or regain hope, unknowingly spiraling deeper into negativity.

Throughout life's journey, you will inevitably face various obstacles, including gates that seem to prevent you from crossing to the other side of despair. These gates can isolate you, trapping you in a prison of fear, insecurity, and loneliness. Yet, no gate is too strong when you are destined to overcome the edge of your circumstances. The truth is, these gates are mere hindrances to the abundance that God has promised you—He will never leave you nor forsake you.

The gate of despair is a result of heavy burdens, disobedience, disappointment, and rebellion against God. Raymond must cross this gate to reach his father's house, even though he fears being consumed by ravenous beasts along the way. Yet, this will not happen because his life has already been divinely orchestrated—he is destined to return to his father's house safely, and no force in hell can prevent that.

In his state of despair, Raymond wonders, *"If I should ever catch a glimpse of my father's home, where I once lived, accustomed to sleeping in comfort and eating good food, I would take a long, deep look into my father's eyes. I wonder if he still has those penetrating eyes that tenderly look into mine and say, 'Raymond, it is well.'"*

Crossing the gate of despair, Raymond experiences a mix of emotions—an unspeakable excitement, a sense of laughter, and an expectation of what lies ahead. It is a road of glorious recovery, and every human being, at least once in their lifetime, must walk it.

At that moment, Raymond could think of nothing positive. He was consumed by feelings of despair, with no light shining to guide his way. He knew his actions against his father had been wrong, and although he felt some opposition to his brother, who might be in a better position and indifferent to him, Raymond made a decision. He would not stay stuck in the pit of self-pity, endlessly pleading *"poor me."* Instead, he decided to rise up, brush off the negativity, and move forward, regardless of what others thought or did.

GATE OF CONFESSIONS

....

If you cover your sins, you shall not prosper. The conditions for obtaining God's mercy are simple and just. They do not require you to perform some grievous act in order to be forgiven. Rather, by confessing your sins to God, who alone has the power to forgive, forgiveness is granted. True confession involves owning up to your wrongdoings, allowing the outpouring of your innermost soul to reach God's infinite mercy.

The spirit of anxiety can greatly hinder your state of mind, leading to extreme stress. It is a mental state driven by concern for something or someone. Anxiety is an obsession that stems from a distorted perspective on life. Therefore, I tell you, do not worry about your life—about what you will eat or drink, or about your body—what you will wear. Is not life more important than food, and the body more important than clothes? Because of the harmful effects of worry, Jesus advises you not to be anxious about these needs, for God promises to supply them. Worry can damage your health and cause the object of your anxiety to consume your thoughts. It will disrupt your productivity and negatively impact how you treat others.

GATE OF REPENTANCE

The gate of repentance is proactive. It involves doing something different—changing direction, and moving away from previous patterns of wrongdoing, especially those things that God hates. Confession is the act of admitting that you have sinned and telling God about your wrongs. Repentance, however, goes beyond just acknowledging sin; it involves feeling regret, contrition, or compunction for what you have done or failed to do. Whether it's a sense of sorrow or a desire for comfort, repentance reflects a change of mind and heart. It is a transformation that engages both the mind and the heart.

GATE OF FORGIVENESS

....

The gate of forgiveness is powerful and strong. It is the pathway to freedom, happiness, communion, and fellowship. Although Raymond believes that he has already asked for forgiveness for his wrongdoings, he must still accept the free gift of forgiveness and walk into the freedom that allows him to bounce back from the edge. Having received forgiveness, Raymond must stop harboring anger toward others. He must forsake his sin and yield himself completely to God. In doing so, he will be restored to full fellowship with God.

Raymond recognizes how forgiveness brings humility and breaks the pride of rebellion and stubbornness. Forgiveness has the power to set one free from the sinful nature that blinds the mind, preventing full awareness of spiritual truths and understanding. Thus, asking for forgiveness is not enough on its own; it must be accompanied by repentance and a commitment to reformation. There must be a deliberate change in life, and all that is offensive to God must be cast aside. Raymond must move on to the gate of self-discovery, guided by the light of God's Word,

His divine will, and the knowledge of the path He desires him to walk.

GATE OF SELF DISCOVERY

Raymond found himself in a destructive situation and desperately needed help. How did he get from where he was? It was a difficult place for someone like him who is coming from a comfortable home. Yet, due to his rebellious behavior, he had ended up there. He was fully aware of his hopelessness and feelings of worthlessness. Despite this, Raymond discovered a better way to confront his mistakes and made a U-turn. He realized that the eye of the Lord was upon him and His ears were open to his cry.

With renewed courage, Raymond recalled, *"The Lord is near to those who have a broken heart and saves those who have a contrite spirit."* This truth encouraged him and gave him a sense of satisfaction in knowing he was not alone. Confronting his low self-esteem, he took heart and moved through this gate with confidence, stepping into a mindset of positivity.

GATE OF ACCEPTANCE

At last, Raymond arrived at the gate of acceptance. He was relieved and had come to his senses. He decided, *"It is well with me, and it is well with my father."* With newfound boldness, Raymond proclaimed, "But as for me, I trust in You, O Lord. My times are in Your hands; make Your face to shine upon me and save me for Your mercy's sake. As many as received You, to them You gave the right to become children of God, to those who believe in Your name. Lord, it is me, Raymond! Surely goodness and mercy shall follow me all the days of my life, and I will dwell in the house of the Lord forever."

Raymond gained confidence and acceptance by asking forgiveness from his earthly father and, more importantly, from his heavenly Father. Reflecting on the pain from his past troubles, he found that it had greatly impacted his mental and emotional stability. The struggle was unbearable at times, raising questions about his willingness to remain in his current situation or to seek and maintain a relationship with God. Although finding God felt like an exhausting and almost impossible experience, Raymond knew that he must continue in faith and keep bouncing back from the edge.

In deep meditation, Raymond accepted, "I cannot demand quick fixes as a way out of my inner turmoil. The weight of my challenges is heavy, and it's hard to find God in the midst of it all. Yet, I must be prepared to exercise patience and a willingness to progress, even in the face of adversity." Raymond realized that God does not deal with men as finite beings deal with one another. His thoughts are full of mercy, love, tenderness, and compassion.

"Let the wicked forsake his way, and the unrighteous his thoughts. Let him return unto the Lord, and He will have mercy upon him, and to our God, for He will abundantly pardon."

The road to recovery is not always paved with gold, success, or opportunities. If it were, you might need to search for it, and when you find it, you must recognize how precious it truly is.

"What is your take on the road you've found yourself on?"
"Where were you before? Were you lost?"

This road is not a common pathway; it is only for those who hope to be rescued. For example, when a driver breaks down, he calls for help from a rescue team, and while waiting for the rescuer's arrival, the recipient's heart is filled with high expectation. When the rescuer finally arrives, the recipient must be prepared to give a clear explanation for why help was needed.

Questions will be asked about the validity of the request, the cause of the breakdown, and once both parties are satisfied with the situation, the recovery process can begin. In Raymond's case, while his father was coming to rescue him, the father had his own expectations. When Raymond's father saw him walking toward him, he instantly recognized his son. Moved with compassion, the father ran toward him without hesitation, eager to embrace his child.

IDENTIFICATION

Raymond had no physical identification, no documents or possessions that could prove who he was, where he came from, or where he was headed. If he ever had such things, they had long been destroyed in the pigpen where he had sunk into despair. He could not respond as energetically as when he had first left his father's house, full of youthful hope and pride. Now, much older, weary, and changed by his experiences, Raymond was almost unrecognizable. His features had altered, and his appearance reflected the toll of his choices. Yet, despite these changes, his father did not need binoculars to spot him from afar. With just one glance, he recognized his son, Raymond.

His outer clothing, ragged and filthy, no longer signified the boy who had once left home in a blaze of self-assurance. It was not the tattered clothes that defined him, but the heart that still carried the love and yearning for home. Similarly, when a sinner comes to Jesus, they are in the filthy rags of sin, unworthy and unclean. Yet, Jesus does not wait for them to clean themselves up; He accepts them as they are. What a profound contrast this is – where the world may judge by appearance and external actions, Jesus sees the heart and offers unconditional acceptance.

This comparison reveals the powerful truth that no matter how far one falls, or how unrecognizable we may seem, God sees beyond the exterior and embraces us with open arms, waiting for our return.

The father's reaction was one of immediate compassion and unconditional love. There was no need for him to question, *"Raymond, is that you?"* or to wait for the son to explain himself. The father recognized him from a distance, without hesitation, and ran to meet him, embracing him with open arms. This was not just a physical reunion, but a profound moment of grace and forgiveness.

For the father, the thought of never seeing his son again had haunted him. Yet, through his persistent prayers and unwavering hope, he had never given up. His prayers were answered not just with the return of his son but with a deeper understanding of love. He had prayed for his son's safe return, and in the moment of their reunion, it was clear that God had heard his prayers.

In this tender moment, the father expressed kindness and acceptance before Raymond even had the chance to confess or repent. It was not the son's repentance that sparked the father's love, but the father's love that opened the door for repentance and healing. This grace-filled response not only restored the son physically, but spiritually as well, as the father showed him that his worth was not based on his past mistakes, but on who he was—his flesh and blood, a child of the father.

Despite the dirt and the stench of the pigpen, the father saw his son for who he truly was, a son who had wandered and strayed, but was now home. The father's unconditional love was a demonstration of how God sees each of us. Just as the father did not allow the filth of sin to define his son, God, through the sacrifice of His Son, demonstrates the same boundless love for us. We are redeemed, not by our own merit, but through the love and grace of our Heavenly Father who, while we were still lost, gave Himself for us.

This reunion was not just about returning to a physical home, but about returning to the true source of belonging, an eternal, unbreakable connection to the father. The father's love was not a fleeting emotion; it was a choice, an act of redemption that brought the son back to life, despite his past mistakes. Just as Jesus' sacrifice on the cross shows His love for us, the father's actions reflect this same love: a love that restores, heals, and welcomes us home no matter how far we've strayed.

The father's heart had been yearning for his son long before that fateful moment when they would meet again. Every night, he prayed, hoping and trusting that one day his son would come home, safe and whole. The father never ceased to think about Raymond, even as he wandered in that far country. His prayers were not driven by anger or resentment but by a deep and unconditional love that transcended Raymond's actions and mistakes. This love was a constant, unyielding force, waiting for the day when the son would return.

When Raymond did return, the father did not hesitate for even a second. He didn't question his son, asking where he had been, what he had done, or why he had stayed away for so long. The father's concern in that moment wasn't about judgment or retribution, but about the deep reunion of a father and his son. The most important thing was that Raymond was home, alive, and the father's love and mercy were enough to heal the wounds of the past. The father's immediate response was to run towards him, not waiting for Raymond to come to him, but taking the initiative to restore the bond that had been broken.

This moment was not by coincidence. It was divine timing, a culmination of prayer, hope, and love that had prepared both father and son for this encounter. Neither of them knew when it would happen or how it would unfold, but both were ready, having endured their own journeys of pain, healing, and growth. The father's heart was in tune with God's love for his son, unfailing and unconditional, always ready to embrace and forgive.

What a powerful and beautiful moment of grace. The father's love was not contingent upon Raymond's actions or worthiness. He didn't need to hear an apology first or see any outward change in Raymond. The love was freely given because Raymond was his son and that was enough. This encounter between father and son exemplifies God's love for His children: always seeking, always welcoming, never counting the past against them, but always ready to embrace them into His fold.

The father's actions in that moment sparks volumes about the nature of divine love. It's not about waiting for perfection or repayment, but about restoration, reconciliation and a love that never gives up. For Raymond, this was not just a physical return home, but a spiritual and emotional homecoming; a return to grace, to peace, and to the loving embrace of a father who had never stopped loving him.

The gracious presentation was an entirely different result from the one the son had envisioned. After a while, father and son walked and talked as close friends. The father never brought up old hurts or broken wounds in their conversation. He was careful not to allow his son to feel regretful while trying to make his way home, being in a fragile state of mind and weakened by physical strength.

The father did his utmost best, handling the situation with care and compassion.

Thus, fathers ought to be very careful in how they win back their sons from the brink of mental turmoil. The tone of their voice when speaking to their son should be compassionate and tender. Even body language can signal whether the father is in a somber mood, speaking quietly in small ways, unlike other times. This brings rest and assurance to a lost son, letting him know, *"It is well now and you will be home, my son."* Sometimes, it takes nothing major to push an individual to the edge of their extremity. All individuals, whether parents or friends, can be much more effective if they swallow their pride and reach out to others in need, preventing a bigger crisis. It's as if they didn't care what happened to the person while they were hurting and lost in life's maze. Instead, go after them, find them, bring them home, and nurse them back into the fold of togetherness, wholeness and (or less whole) harmony in the family.

There is a safe place called home, especially a place children long to return to. Home is where love is plentiful, protection is secure, peace is cherished and there is an attitude of caring and sharing. It is a place of laughter, giving and taking and sometimes not passing the blame on others. After confessing your guilt, prayer should be for inner renewal and thanksgiving, leading to recovery by overcoming several gates.

When Raymond's father saw him and began running toward him, he didn't mind tripping and falling. Surely, he would have happily gotten up again and kept running toward his son, whom he thought he would never see again. He thought, *"He is alive, thank God!"* The father continued praying and thanking God for the safe return of his son. He hugged his son with a tender embrace, as if to say, *"My son, do you know how many nights I have envisioned this moment, hugging and kissing you?"* His spirit was overwhelmed.

Though the father had aged from the stress his son caused when he left home, his aging feet broke through all protocols as he ran and fell upon his son's neck. Despite feeling guilty and deserving of punishment, the father welcomed his son with open arms. Though the son wore ragged, dirty clothes from feeding pigs, the father took him into his arms, laid him on his cchest and kissed him. This kiss not only assured him of a warm welcome but sealed his pardon, saying that his past mistakes were forgiven without a single word of reproach.

The father did not express any word of rebuke towards his son though the son came home in rags and unrecognizable. His father did not only clothed him, but adorned him with the best robe said to his servants.

"Bring out the best robe and put it on him."

The best robe was the principal robe to be put on him. Though he might have been ashamed to wear it, he was clothed in it because he had come home in such a dirty state. The robe symbolized the father's love and affection toward his son. Putting a ring on his hand, which was a signet ring, bearing the arms of the family. It served as a token of being welcomed back and recognized as part of the family again.

The ring would serve as a memorial of his father's kindness, reminding him never to forget it. Raymond had come home barefoot, perhaps with sore feet from his long journey. Now, he was no longer barefoot or hungry. His father didn't just feed him, he gave him a feast, ordering the fatted calf to be killed so that his son could be satisfied with the best they had. The fatted calf was a symbol of festive celebration and rejoicing for Raymond's long-awaited return. It was to be killed and prepared for this joyful occasion. This act did not mean that the father's love for his son depended on his faithfulness; no, it was an unconditional love. Even when Raymond was a wanderer, wasting his time and money in riotous living, his father loved him.

Raymond reflected, *"My former employer hired me to feed pigs,"* a degrading job that was unfit for someone like him. But it wasn't the employer's fault, it was his own. He had lived a worthless life and now he had gotten what he deserved. Raymond thought about the time when he lived at home as a prince, enjoying the comforts of his father's house. Now life had brought him to a much lower state. He had once been used to commanding the servants, but now, he longed to be a servant himself.

Raymond was lost for words and couldn't recall what he had rehearsed to say to his father when he arrived home. The words seemed to come automatically, just as he was about to speak. He had rehearsed saying to his father, *"I have sinned against heaven and in your sight, I am no longer worthy to be called your son. Make me like one of your hired servants."*

Nevertheless, the real challenge goes beyond mere words; it requires active action, bouncing back from the edge to avoid falling over. In life, we must take the good with the bad and prioritize the best options for success. Sometimes, we smile even when we are feeling sad. We love what we have, remembering what we had, always forgive and never forget when people change. Things will go wrong, but we must remember to ride through the storm (unknown author).

Would you willingly give your inheritance to your young and irresponsible son, as Raymond had requested? Consider the nature of Raymond's attitude while traveling along this wide, broad and unknown path, where he may encounter many obstacles, potholes, landslides and hindrances in his way. If he truly desires to reach his destination, he must make up his mind to find ways to overcome each challenge, dealing with every conflict inch by inch along the way. Life is not handed to anyone on a platter and Raymond will need to search diligently for the right path. Once he finds it, he must walk in it carefully.

If circumstances drive you near danger, it is advisable to look for a way out. If life pushes you to the edge, find a way to step back from it. Whether you walk, run, or slide away from danger, take nothing for granted and leave nothing to chance. Find a way out or over to the safe path. Sadly, if you fall, you might be able to get up on your own, but at times, you may need someone to help you up. Your circumstances may be beyond your control, but your character is not. Therefore, you cannot blame your character flaws on your circumstances, just as you wouldn't blame a mirror for the reflection it shows.

What you see in the mirror is yourself and no one else. A person with integrity will always strive to make positive, clean choices. Every time you make a decision based on your values, you take a step forward in your spiritual growth. Raymond had time to reflect on the many destructive elements he had faced and where he currently stood. He named each stage of his journey as a positive entrance, a way of bouncing back from the edge. He happily declared, *"I have made it back from the edge of my circumstances with the help of God."*

"Though I walk through the valley of the shadow of death, I will fear no evil, for You are with me; Your rod and Your staff, they comfort me." Therefore, embrace and respect your identity as a child of the King. The birth of Jesus, your Heavenly Father, shows God's incredible love for you, to participate in every aspect of your life, not for what you did, but simply because you are His child.

PRAYER

Thank You, Lord, for Your compassionate love and mercy, Heavenly Father. Though I have abused Your love and squandered the blessings You have given me, I will arise and go to my Father and say, "I have sinned against heaven and before You, and I am no longer worthy to be called Your son. Make me like one of Your hired servants" (Luke 15:18-20).

BOUNCING BACK FROM THE EDGE

Chapter 8

CONFRONTING FEAR

Confronting the destructive spirit of fear can be an unpleasant, dangerous and painful emotional experience. To confront the spirit of fear, one must first understand what fear is. Fear has many definitions, but at its core, it is an emotional response to a perceived threat to one's security or general well-being. It ranges in intensity from mild anxiety or worry to overwhelming terror. However, fear can also be a useful emotion when it prompts appropriate caution or actions that protect one's welfare.

A cause of fear is anxiety, a feeling of deep uneasiness that leads to worry, apprehension, or even dread. Fear can manifest as a negative force at any stage of an individual's life. It may present as a subtle, gnawing uneasiness or as a paralyzing emotion that disrupts breathing and immobilizes the mind and body. On the other hand, fear can become a significant hindrance to the enjoyment of life if it overwhelms positive emotions such as love and joy. When fear dominates, it may lead to an inability to engage in normal, everyday activities, thereby diminishing one's quality of life.

Fear is often associated with an expectation of harm or pain, typically experienced as a painful emotion characterized by alarm, dread and unease. However, fear can also take the form of a calm recognition or consideration of potential dangers that might cause injury or damage. This kind of recognition prompts reasonable caution and intelligent foresight.

Christians are instructed to cultivate godly fear, a reverential fear that is considered the beginning of wisdom. As Scripture teaches, God has not given Christians a spirit of fear but one of power, love, and a sound mind. The proper fear of God is essential for those who seek to serve Him. This is not a morbid or crippling fear but rather a profound respect and reverence. The fear of God involves hating what is bad and turning away from evil, as Proverbs 16:6 states: *"By the fear of the Lord, one departs from evil."*

The fears faced by young people, while not as numerous or overwhelming as those that often arise later in life, can still be significant. In youth, self-confidence, energy and diverse interests often help minimize fears. However, as life progresses, firsthand experiences with failure, illness, or other hardships can heighten fear. For instance, after enduring a serious illness, one might develop a fear of being unable to meet the demands of daily life, which can erode peace of mind.

One of humanity's greatest fears is the fear of death. However, we are assured that perfect love casts out all fear. The believing fear of God acts as a safeguard against the unsettling fear of man. As Paul explains, "For God gave us not a spirit of fear, but of power, love, and soundness of mind." This teaches us that we should strive to learn from our mistakes and make efforts not to repeat them. If you find yourself fearing the future of the world, remember that God holds the past, present and future in His hands.

Victims who find themselves brought to the edge often experience overwhelming fear, unsure whether they will be rescued or bounce back from their difficult circumstances. Why do people fear so many things or become afraid of making mistakes? The answer lies in Scripture: *"Trust in the Lord with all your heart and lean not on your own understanding; in all your ways, acknowledge Him, and He will direct your path"* (Proverbs 3:5-6).

The principles of fear are also addressed in Isaiah 8:12, where God cautions His people against the sin of fear. Fear was prevalent among the people and He reminded them that fear is contagious. Instead, He advised them to embrace a reverent, religious fear, to sanctify the Lord of hosts. Allowing others to intimidate you can neutralize your effectiveness for God.

Discover how the power of the Holy Spirit can help you overcome fear. As 2 Timothy 1:7 reminds us, God equips us with the strength to rise above fear and continue doing His will: *"For God has not given us a spirit of fear, but of power, love, and a sound mind."*

The entire duty of man is to fear God and keep His commandments. When God is the object of fear, this may involve terror, honor and submission, accompanied by a profound sense of worship. For those who are enemies of the Lord rather than His followers, terror is the most appropriate response. However, such terror is tempered by the fact that God is not capricious; He acts consistently according to His righteous character and revealed will.

Nevertheless, those who are guilty of idolatry and injustice have every reason to fear His coming wrath.

For believers, the proper attitude toward God is often described as respect, reverence, or awe rather than fear. However, the biblical terminology for this attitude frequently uses the same word for *'fear'* and God's character remains unchanged. In fact, the descriptions of God often translated as *'awesome'* are literally rendered as *'feared'* or *'fearful'* (see Exodus 15:11).

THE CAUSE OF FEAR

The spirit of fear is like a mask, concealing its true identity and presenting false evidence that appears real but is not. Fear is often caused by disobedience. For instance, when Adam sinned, he experienced fear. When God called to him in the garden, saying, *"Where are you?"* Adam replied, *"I heard Your voice in the garden and I was afraid because I was naked, so I hid myself"* (see Genesis 3:9-10).

INVASION OF DOUBTS

....

The invasion of doubts is often caused by Satan, unbelief, worldly wisdom and spiritual instability. However, God has never asked us to believe without providing sufficient evidence on which to base our faith. For example, His existence, character and the truthfulness of His Word are supported by testimony that appeals to reason. Yet, God has also not removed the possibility of doubt, ensuring that faith rests on evidence rather than absolute demonstration.

When the Word of God is approached without reverence or prayer and ones thoughts and affections are not aligned with God's will, the mind becomes clouded with doubt. In such moments, the enemy seizes control of thoughts, offering false interpretations that lead to confusion. Doubts, at their core, are uncertainties of the mind.

There are two kinds of doubt:

1. **Uncertainty**—a genuine questioning, stemming from an honest search for truth and a lack of clarity about what to believe.

2. **Distrustful doubt**—a more negative form, involving suspicion and skepticism that undermines belief in truth or positive interactions.

It is important to recognize how easily one can slip from honest uncertainty into outright unbelief if doubts are left unchecked.

For example, the less you read God's Word and pray, the more you begin to trust your own judgment. This can lead to doubts and perplexities. Doubts have many causes, such as fear of failure, prolonged painful situations, or confronting a strong enemy like Satan. To handle doubt, you must not deny its existence. Instead, face your doubts honestly and confess them to God.

A wise approach involves examining yourself for unconfessed sins or other hindrances. Believe that God is greater than your problems and fully capable of guiding you through your doubts. When faced with the choice of bouncing back from the edge or giving up, trust in His power to see you through.

The best and most effective solution to overcoming doubt is developing a firm belief in God. By building a strong relationship with Him and trusting in who He is, you can replace the spirit of doubt with unwavering faith. This relationship will bring relief from doubt and transform fear into trust.

In the natural world, you are constantly surrounded by mysteries that you cannot fully comprehend. Even the simplest forms of life present challenges that the wisest educators are powerless to explain beyond superficial knowledge. However, studying the Word of God sheds light on the deeper problems, including the issue of doubt.

Approaching God's Word with an attitude of respect and submission, sometimes referred to as fear, carries with it the expectation of obedience. This respect or reverence is also the proper attitude toward God's sanctuary. In Scripture, the honor associated with *'fear'* is evident in how Israel revered God. In this sense, fear stands in direct opposition to treating someone or something as common, insignificant, irreverent, or unworthy of attention *(see related applications in health and spiritual well-being)*.

Chapter 9

FACING HEALTH ISSUES

Though tears are often defined as drops flowing from the eyes, they can be triggered by various causes. They may result from irritants or laughter, but are most commonly associated with weeping, sorrow and grief. When you cry, friends wonder what's wrong and try to console you. Babies cry for food, children cry when they lose a pet and adults cry when confronted with trauma and death.

There are various physical illnesses that affect individuals, causing suffering throughout their lives, some of which are critical or serious. Whatever the case, every bodily illness casts certain fears upon the human mind and can keep a person in bondage, fighting fatigue and distress in one way or another. When a person is diagnosed with a critical illness, some may feel as though they are already dead.

There is no comfort at the edge, whether you are in the midst of life's challenges, simply strolling along, or sitting and waiting to be rescued. In such moments, it's often worthwhile to cry out *"Help,"* hoping someone will come to your aid. No individual, no matter how good or great, is exempt from the arrest of sickness and the inevitability of death.

Katie, a young and prosperous woman, was experiencing serious health issues and was on the brink of losing her life. She was miraculously brought back from the edge. On more than one occasion, she felt as though death was knocking at her door, seeking entrance. Despite these hopeless circumstances, she never gave up hope. This intelligent, beautiful and popular woman was outgoing, in her prime and loving life to the fullest when suddenly, poor health struck. She was diagnosed and her entire world seemed to collapse, leading her to what appeared to be a dead end.

The uncertainty was inevitable. With a good job, she didn't hesitate to seek medical help early, receiving immediate attention that brought her back from the edge. Katie was elated and grateful, sharing her story with others. She desired to survive, yet she was also acutely aware of the potential costs and the possibility that it might not work out.

Katie was faced with a decision: to live or to die. She developed a strong desire to pray and reach out to God, allowing her mind to focus on the luxury of feeling optimistic and confident about bouncing back from the edge. She visualized herself alive, given another chance to start over and felt passionate about living as if stepping into a new world. She sought the right path and committed to walking in it.

She decided to focus on doing the right things, thinking about things that are lovely, peaceful, pure and true. With the help of a medical team, praying friends and her own renewed mindset, Katie's mind was stabilized through meditation, the prayers of God's people and the intervention of doctors. Yet, she knew that each person must remain obedient and committed to following instructions to aid in their recovery. With a made-up mind, she chose to do what was advisable in sound wisdom.

RECOVERY

Thankfully, Katie made a full recovery from the serious illness that nearly brought her to the edge of the unknown. She is now alive to share her story, continuing to bounce back to a better life of healing and deliverance. It is important to keep the mind fresh and free from the pollution of anger, hate and selfishness. Through positive actions and surrounding herself with positive people and the right company, Katie proved that it is indeed possible to bounce back from the edge of serious illness, an illness that could have led her to a point of no return.

MENTAL ILLNESS

Not many people are able to cope with life's challenges after recovering from a traumatic condition, especially a serious mental illness. Mental health struggles are not a sign of weakness, but rather a condition that can affect anyone, regardless of strength or resilience. Mental illness knows no boundaries, it can affect the young and old, the rich andpoor and both men and women. It is a global epidemic, impacting cultures and societies everywhere.

Individuals may struggle with mental health issues at various stages of their lives, often for different reasons. Ricardo, a 20-year-old young man, was a prime example. He was independent, but his life took a turn when he was suddenly expelled from school due to his bad attitude toward classmates and teachers. He found it difficult to cope and blamed others for driving him to this point. Despite this, he refused to seek help or adhere to counseling. When he was wrong, he would defend himself fiercely, insisting on his innocence.

Ricardo was unknowingly developing mental health issues, but it was evident in his behavior. He began to isolate himself from his friends, constantly wanting to be left alone. His neglect of personal hygiene and his disregard for changing clothes were noticeable. Previously tidy, he now seemed indifferent to his appearance and well-being. This behavior, though not yet diagnosed by a doctor, signaled a deeper issue that needed attention.

One afternoon, Ricardo met Sam, someone who seemed to be in a similar situation. They were introduced to an older friend who suggested they take a trip away from home to escape and relax without disturbances. The two friends decided to travel by night, hoping their whereabouts would go unnoticed. However, by the time they reached their destination, it was very late and they realized it wasn't such a good idea after all. Unfortunately, they had no money for transportation and couldn't return home.

Feeling trapped and regretting their decision, they found an old barn and decided to sleep there for the night. As darkness fell, they tried to make the best of the situation. Ricardo, who was more resourceful than Sam, went to a local takeaway and begged for food. To his surprise, he was granted some.

On the second night, with no proper assistance to deal with their growing mental health struggles, the two boys were acting strangely. Someone noticed their awkward behavior and approached them. This Good Samaritan suggested that they visit a local counselor, not far from where they were staying, to seek the help they desperately needed.

The boys, desperate for help and relief, agreed to accept the offer. They willingly embraced the challenge of seeking help, which included medical checkups, counseling, a

Facing Health Issues

clean place to stay, food, and fresh clothes for a period of four weeks.

During their stay, the boys were asked to reflect on what led them to this state of mind. At first, they didn't realize the seriousness of their condition, but it became clear that both were struggling with mental health issues. While not severe at the time, it was a significant concern.

Each day, they were monitored and tested to ensure that the treatment was effectively addressing their mental health needs. By the end of the four weeks, both boys were grateful to have escaped the trap at the edge of mental illness.

One day, Ricardo had a heartfelt conversation with Sam. They agreed that it was time to return home and confess to their parents about the poor decisions they had made by straying from a comfortable and supportive home. It was time to leave the uncomfortable surroundings and head back to their families.

The boys were fortunate to have the means to get home safely and after a long journey, they finally arrived and parted ways. Sam said, *"Alright, mate, let's meet at the large tree tomorrow around the corner."*

Ricardo responded, *"Okay, Sam. I'll see what happens after my mum finishes drilling me for answers about where I've been for the past six weeks. Maybe I'll tell her something… but the truth?"*

Sam raised an eyebrow, *"I can't tell the truth. My dad will kill me. Honestly, my parents never believe anything I say anyway."*

Ricardo reminded him of the counselor's advice: *"Always tell the truth. Otherwise, your mental health will suffer. It'll gnaw at you, and holding onto a lie will only make things worse. Let's be honest and own up to what we've done."*

Sam, after a pause, responded, *"Yeah, you're right. That's a better idea."*

The boys decided not to meet up again for five days, not wanting to raise any suspicion with their parents. However, when the truth eventually came out, their parents were more understanding than they had expected. They recognized the struggles the boys had been going through and, instead of reacting harshly, contacted the authorities and made plans to support them with ongoing counseling.

Though their mental health issues had been mild at the time, it was clear they could have escalated if left unchecked. Mental health challenges among young people are widespread and many can face them without even realizing how serious they might become.

The story ended on a positive note: the boys' parents decided to support them, acknowledging that, despite the severity of their behavior, they were fortunate that things hadn't taken a darker turn. Society often overlooks early signs of mental health issues, but both boys had been lucky to catch their problems in time.

The message is clear: if you notice someone behaving out of character, approach them gently and encourage them to seek help before it's too late. Mental illness is not a problem to be taken lightly, it can lead to tragic consequences if not addressed early. Many lives have been lost due to the negligence of recognizing and treating mental health issues.

As a society, especially in this era, we must be vigilant and mindful of the welfare of others. Keep an eye out for those who may be struggling and don't let another victim fall through the cracks of neglect when it comes to mental health.

Regardless of whether a disease manifests physically or mentally, illnesses that limit human function and reduce the quality of life can be overwhelming. The successful treatment of these diseases relies primarily on prompt and accurate diagnosis, along with the use of effective therapeutic methods.

Unfortunately, in biblical times, people had limited means to diagnose and treat illnesses. Even the most educated individuals had only a rudimentary understanding of human anatomy and physiology, and their knowledge of diseases and their effects on the body was minimal. The concept of bacteria and viruses was unknown and many health conditions were often attributed to supernatural causes, such as sin or curses from enemies.

In those times, healing and health restoration often involved spiritual or ritualistic practices, with the belief that disease could be a divine judgment or a consequence of wrong actions. People sought remedies from religious leaders, priests, or healers, but modern medicine as we know it today was not yet developed.

PRAYER

....

Dear God, thank You for granting wisdom and understanding as we navigate through the twists and turns of life. Please help me to put You first for Your name's sake. I ask for courage to reach out to individuals who may be suffering from the deadly disease of mental health. Father, You are our Healer; heal Your people, O Lord. Your Word declares, "If My people who are called by My name will humble themselves and pray, turn from their wicked ways and seek My face, then I will hear from heaven and heal their land." Thank You for healing our land. In Jesus' mighty name, Amen.

BOUNCING BACK FROM THE EDGE

Chapter 10

BOUNCE TO FREEDOM

Whether fleeing oppression, stepping out of prison, breaking a strangling habit, or bouncing back from the edge, freedom means life. There is nothing more exhilarating than knowing that the past is forgiven and new options await. People yearn to be free.

Freedom is the release from bondage, the lifting of the weight of guilt and shame. The individual granted freedom will feel lightness in their steps as they bounce back to life once more. There will be no more condemnation; it has been rolled over the edge of adversity. It takes courage and expectation to journey from a distant place to the destination you've always visualized in your dreams. Sometimes, it feels like you're walking in a dream, especially when you're walking on foot toward your desired destination.

You may have experienced unbearable cuts and bruises, painful joints, dehydration, tiredness and delusions. Regrets will surface and negative thoughts may flood your mind. Yet, despite the bruises inflicted by daily interactions, you may feel like giving in after reaching the edge.

You are advised to hang in there and swim against the flow. There may be setbacks, but nothing will prevent you from bouncing back from the edge. It will feel like a forgotten dream, just keep reaching out.

The challenge of receiving freedom can be shared with others, whether within a family unit or among a community. This freedom can be used to build the life you long for, a life determined not by external pressures, but by a life of togetherness.

For instance, Raymond was on the right path, in his right mind. The very thought of the distance from home was daunting and yet, negativity suddenly emerged, tempting him to give up and lie down. During fierce battles, challenges and severe temptations between pressing on and withdrawing, Raymond found the courage to reflect: I must fight to resist distractions and attractions, and keep moving forward. Even when feeling fainthearted, he reminded himself that he must find fresh motivation for a brighter future. He kept bouncing back, pursuing against all odds, refusing to give up the chase and following steadfastly toward his destination, his father's house, as if nothing else mattered.

Most people are privileged to travel by motor vehicle, bicycle, or with the help of animals to assist their journey. But in Raymond's case, he had to journey on foot from where he found himself to his father's house. He had wasted all his money, was broke and could not afford transportation. The weather, too, was out of hiscontrol, whether it was bright and sunny or rainy, he had no say. With little to carry but the rags on his back, Raymond carried a heavy load: a broken, painful heart and the unbearable weight of his sin.

On his journey, as he neared the point of bouncing back from the edge, a strong wind of adversity blew his way, nearly pushing him back to the edge from where he started. The wind was so fierce that it tossed and shook him side to side, finally knocking him off his feet and into the ground. He mumbled, *"That's my payment for rebelling against my father's authority. God sometimes settles debts without money. An old saying, but I believe it's true. Still, I'm depending on His mercy."* With strong determination, he rose, brushed himself off and continued bouncing back.

It was a blessing that no one saw him lying in the mud. Perhaps they would have shouted, *"Good for you! What you've sown, that's what you're reaping, disobedient boy! The way of the rebellious is hard!"* Raymond refused to listen to the voices of condemnation. *"If that's you, Satan, you dream killer, get away,"* he mumbled. *"I'm not listening to anyone who hasn't walked in my shoes or been where I've been. I'll keep bouncing back from the edge. Soon enough, I'll be home with my father."*

It was indeed a wonderful moment when Raymond took the initiative to console himself against the negative thoughts plaguing his mind. He held it together, understanding that it wasn't always easy to keep going, but the desire to return home gave him the strength. It is one thing to bounce up and down through rain or sunshine, but it's a whole different challenge when fighting against the elements and your own doubts.

On the other hand, it can be more difficult for individuals in a disturbed state of mind to think positively. But what if it's the other way around? What if someone, at the end of their emotional strength, breaks down? Their journey of bouncing back from the edge to freedom might include crossing bridges of health issues, facing life-threatening circumstances and waiting for the results of medical examinations.

Raymond decided to bounce back home, through hell and high waters and perhaps, if he got too close to the edge, he might accidentally fall over. After all, many have tragically not returned to tell their story. *"Who wants that?"* he thought. *"If not for the prayers of my father and the mercies of God, I wouldn't be in a position to bounce back from the edge."*

Raymond knew life may not be the same as when he left home, but he was determined to give it his best shot, to go back home to his father who had never stopped loving him. Even though he had acted irresponsibly and made foolish decisions that got him into big trouble, trouble that was nearly unforgivable, he still had hope.

"Although my father was deeply disappointed when I rebelled against him and though he may never forget, he will never give up on me. Through rain or sunshine, my father will be there for me," Raymond reflected confidently.

He thought his father might be dead, and he too, could have been dead, perhaps from some misfortunate circumstance, or even eaten by stray animals while in the pig pen. But he hopefully declared, *"Though I was lost, now I am found by my father. He came himself looking for me. My father could have sent my brother or one of his hired servants to search for me, but no, my father came himself."*

Raymond was confident of the love of his father and that gave him more enthusiasm to continue bouncing back to his father's home from the edge of life atrocities until he was home at last in his father's care. He recalled the joyful and memorable day came when he met with his father face to face reunited, he who cares and longed for his son returning safely, his arms were stretched wide open wide, in forgiveness and acceptance; he has never driven his son away.

They both waited in anticipation for that golden moment, one that would go down in the record of history, a loving father reaching out to his wayward unruly son, until he found him safe and sound. Everyone should have their own testimony of how they bounced back from the edge of sin into the loving arms of Jesus, their heavenly Father. There are times when you walk away from something valuable and precious and it can be emotionally heart-wrenching, especially when you feel it was of great value or importance to you.

There are places or things you may walk away from and at times, you might feel the urge to return, seeking freedom. It takes humility during your most difficult times and your stability comes from the presence of peace, so you can walk into the future with confidence. Raymond often remembered, "There was no reaping of food in its season from the land where famine reigns, where it holds the title of king but yields neither food nor water for the welfare of its people."

The land became dry and parched and the trees withered due to the lack of freshness and rain to quench the thirst of both man and beast.

'Why did he settle in this place?

When an individual is in a state of rebellion, their way of thinking becomes toxic and they begin to believe that everyone around them is rebelling as well. The thought process of such an individual doesn't function normally; suspicion and blame are set in their mind, always looking for victims of past mistakes.

Then, Raymond came to his senses and made his way home to his father, carrying the positive assurance that his father was still alive and would receive him when he arrived. Yet, in the back of Raymond's mind, he pondered the decision he made when he left his father's home. What if that had caused his father so much pain that he became ill and might have passed away? But that did not happen.

It was indeed a long road from the bondage of the edge to the freedom where Raymond decided to bounce back to, maintaining his stride as if bouncing like a ball, trying to get into a groove. His mind reflected on the time when he fed the pigs and found no pleasure in it and now he had an important task ahead of him, fulfilling his desire to return home.

Raymond picked up speed, keeping pace as if in a hurry to attend an important event or receive the prize of *'well done.'* He made strides more effectively, with home in view and the anticipation of meeting and greeting his longed-for, loving father. Without strong determination, combined with his father's prayers, Raymond would have fallen over the edge of his depravity. Or, another deadly edge, such as mental health struggles, could have caught him without warning. This can become so consuming that you focus on one idea long enough, without seeing or dreaming of a way out and before you know it, you've gone over the edge.

Raymond was fortunate that such a fate did not befall him while he was talking to himself and feeding the pigs. He rejoiced and shouted loudly, *"That was my yesterday. I'm in a new world of positive thinking, things are looking up."* Raymond had a new vision and new expectations. He reflected, *"Perhaps it was good for me to be driven to this place of adversity; otherwise, I might never have realized or understood the worth of my father's prayers."*

Despite his reflections, Raymond was willing to return home, even as a servant. He was surprised when his father accepted him back as his son, as if he had never gone astray. *"Oh, the love of a loving father, it passes human understanding! How do they do it? How well do they execute love toward the right person, at the right time? It's unbelievable!"*

Through all of Raymond's failures, he had been desperately lacking wisdom from the outset. A man without wisdom and grace, though he plans in the end, will become a fool and will have no right to true joy. Therefore, it is important to gain wisdom and knowledge. Those who do so show that they love their soul and they will find that they have done the greatest kindness imaginable.

STUCK BEYOND THE EDGE

The fortitude to help oneself out of despondency is a powerful thing. A story is told of a man who sat by a pool for years, waiting for someone to help him into the water. He asked his friends to escort him each day because he was unable to walk on his own. The man had heard that a miracle would occur at certain times when the water in the pool would be stirred and the first person to step in would be healed of any disease. Yet, he made no attempt to help himself, as he was mentally incapacitated.

He might not have even shown any signs that he desired help to be placed in the pool. He wasn't accustomed to helping himself or asking for help. He did nothing, not even shuffling himself closer to the edge of the pool. Despite having the ambition to be healed, he did nothing to rescue himself from his situation.

One day, a Good Samaritan came along and asked him, "Do you want to be made whole?" The man answered, *"I have no one to help me into the pool or to take me away from the edge."* The Good Samaritan then ordered, *"Rise up, take up your mat and walk home."*

This man was seen as unequipped, uninspired and paralyzed. Not in his body, but in his mindset, his moods, and his ability to move forward to a better place. Perhaps he had given up a long time ago without saying a word. Could it be that he had been cast down by the mockery of others, told that he would never get better, that he would die in his condition? He seemed hopeless, useless and good for nothing.

Do you know someone in such a desperate condition?

Many people behave like this man, procrastinating and putting off the urge to help themselves. Although he had a mouth to ask for help, hands to signal for assistance and eyes to see passersby, he did nothing, just sitting at the edge of the pool, waiting to be moved. If only he had done what needed to be done today, instead of making excuses without changing his behaviour, this would be manipulation.

The nameless man was eventually rescued and taken back from the edge. Although the road to recovery was long and rough, there was still hope, thanks to God's mercy. He had personal ambitions to accomplish many things in life, but he lacked the ability to help himself. Without making an effort to help himself, he would always be dependent on others, shifting from one place to the next. Instead, he needed to try his best, not to become like everyone else, but to be himself and watch the changes that come from trying.

The man obeyed what he was told to do. He took up his mat and bounced back joyfully from the edge; he was delighted. He reflected on the many times he had wanted to move but was always trying to get in before someone else when the angel came down to stir the water. Now, he was free to walk and bounce back from the edge of despair.

The man needed wisdom, the ability to put knowledge to work or use, which is the intelligent application for the benefit of learning. For instance, a person might have considerable knowledge but not know how to use it due to a lack of understanding or the ability to see how different aspects of something relate to one another. To see the entire picture, not just isolated facts, that is good understanding. A person with understanding is able to connect new information to things he already knows. Therefore, knowledge and understanding are allied and both should be sought. (Proverbs 2:5, 18:15)

RAYMOND'S PRAYER

Dear God, thank You for the mindset to bounce back from where I was to where I am heading. Had it not been for Your mercies, this would not be possible. Thank You for Your faithfulness toward me. I was like a lost man, heading nowhere, but I'm so glad You found me and turned my life around.

Father God, may I always remember Your goodness throughout my entire life as I make my way back to my Father's house. In Jesus' name, Amen.

BOUNCING BACK FROM THE EDGE

Chapter 11

HOME SWEET HOME

A home is the center of family life. It is a place where things like eating, homemaking, religious training, entertainment, and domestic counsel take place. It is also where God's blessings and wisdom are shared. Home is where families live together, rejuvenating their rhythms and prayers, and seeking ways to reach out to God in times of anxiety. It is a space where families engage more frequently and intentionally with God and one another.

Home is where families share togetherness and establish regular morning conversations about life—both present and future. It is a place where freedom exists within constraints, and where one can begin building the life God desires.

As Raymond anticipated returning home, he made plans for how he would behave, particularly in his attitude, daily communication, and interactions with his father and brother. He decided he would conduct himself wisely. Reflecting, he thought, *"I've blown out all my candles through ignorance."*

He resolved, *"I will be extremely cautious in everything I do and say."* Raymond knew that people from the community would be visiting his father's house, inquiring about what had happened to the runaway son and voicing their opinions on how they would have treated him if they were in his father's place.

"Thank God, they are not my father," he thought. *"My father is a good dad—a patient and loving father."*

Although his father did not send servants to search for him when he left, he came looking for him himself. *"My heart will beat more than a thousand drums put together,"* Raymond reflected. He realized that sharing his story might help other young boys, like himself, learn an important lesson about avoiding the same foolish mistake—leaving the comfort and stability of their father's house to chase the temporary happiness of the world.

Nevertheless, my desire is to share my experience with those I come into contact with, offering a warning to guard against all kinds of greed. I've learned the hard way that this leads to a life of covetousness, disaffection, and a desire to get rich as quickly as possible. Raymond said to himself, *"When I left home with my inheritance, I thought I could make a life on my own, better than what my father provided with his resources and guidance. Being young, full of energy and skills, I believed I could do it all. But I was mistakenly misguided. I lacked the wisdom of God and didn't know how to handle the ups and downs of life as my father did."*

Leaving my comfort zone and stepping out of line, I didn't know I would be tested and pushed to heights I once thought were beyond my reach. I surpassed even those with greater talent who settled for status, yet I went further than them. Even though on the outside it often seemed like things were falling apart, I took courage and didn't give in, nor did I fall over the edge of my current situation. Instead, I kept my thoughts focused on home.

Raymond rehearsed, *"After all, I'm not living under the old ways of feeding pigs anymore. I'm anticipating a new life. It was easier to give way to despair and self-pity than to go back to school and train for a new career. It takes guts to stand up for my convictions when I'm under fire, but now that I'm nearly home, I'll need to readjust my thinking and relearn good habits and behaviors. It will be beneficial, not just for me, but for all who come into my space."*

He was truly repentant and thought, *"I will resist the old system that led me to run away from my father's house. I will pray for the renewing of my mind every day, reflecting on where I was before I ran away. By praying, meditating, reading my Bible, and focusing on things that are lovely, good, and pleasant, I must never give up on myself. I must not be proud or stubborn, thinking I know it all just because of my youth."*

"I must seek daily peace with my father and often tell him how much I love and appreciate him. I must thank my father for praying for me even when I was out of his sight. Now, I realize how much my gratitude means to him. I will never let a day pass without praising and worshipping my heavenly Father, as well as my earthly father. Both are important in my life."

Though my earthly father is visible to me and I can see and touch him, my heavenly Father is the key. He gives both my father and me life. It was a strange and surprising scene when Raymond and his father walked through the family home. Both were tired and hungry from the long journey back. His father not only fed him but feasted him, ordering that the fatted calf be brought and killed so that his son could be satisfied with the best he had.

It was a great privilege for the son, who had once filled his belly with husks, to see his words come true: *"In my father's house there is bread enough and to spare."* He reflected on how, when his father ordered the fatted calf to be brought out, it was intended as a feast for him. But it turned into a celebration for the entire family. There was so much food that others were invited to come and enjoy the feast. Joy filled the atmosphere, and it was the father who initiated the festivities, setting everyone else to rejoice. So, they all began to be merry. The father rejoiced that his son, whom he thought was lost, was alive and in his right mind, able to recognize the goodness and mercies of God, who had kept him safe and brought him home from the edge.

INSIDE CONFLICTS

While the rejoicing inside the house was going on, an unexpected problem arose: the elder brother, Ronald, was resentful and envious. He complained that he had always been good and never strayed like his younger brother. The older son valued his own higher privileges and despised his brother, who had squandered his portion. He felt superior and self-righteous, now understandably annoyed that his brother had been lavished with mercy and kindness.

The eldest son was vocal in airing his grievance and refused to join in the celebration. He lamented that he had never had a feast, a small celebration with his friends, which he thought would be more modest. He spoke of his brother with disdain, not acknowledging him as his brother, but as a stranger: *"This thy son, who has squandered your inheritance!"*

When the father saw his eldest son's reaction, he was deeply surprised. He hadn't realized that his son harbored such selfishness and bitterness toward his brother—who had been lost and now returned home safely. The father, however, gently comforted his son, saying, *"Son, you are always with me, and everything I have is yours. Why do you allow such feelings to overtake you?"*

This is a sad truth—some families or even best friends struggle to celebrate when someone else is in the spotlight, especially when favor is given to others. They refuse to rejoice in others' blessings, preferring the attention to always be on themselves. The selfish attitude of Ronald reflects how deeply he was hurting, consumed by resentment and jealousy, with no compassion for the rescue of his younger brother from the edge of destruction.

Ronald had the greatest privilege of being in his father's home, enjoying life's blessings, never having to share his portion with his younger brother. He may not have been happy when Raymond decided to leave, but he could have shown some compassion for his brother's safe return. Instead, his behavior mirrored that of a Pharisee—selfish, always about *"me, me, me."* There's often a hidden issue in the heart, and it only takes a small spark for it to be exposed. This issue can manifest anywhere, at any time, without warning. It's like a hidden stream, waiting for the rain to fill its banks, only to flush out unwanted bitterness, jealousy, and envy—habits that block the flow of grace and joy.

Ronald acted like a naughty child, throwing a tantrum when visitors were invited to the house. He was like the bedbugs that only reveal themselves when they're in the best company, making a scene when things were meant to be joyous. The eldest brother's foolishness and fretfulness became evident upon the reception of his brother. At the time of the celebration, he was out in the field, unaware of the homecoming. By the time he returned, the sounds of joy drew near and he heard music and dancing.

Such a celebration had never been seen before in the house, and he asked what was going on. He was informed that his brother had come home and their father had prepared a great feast to welcome him, filled with joy because his son was safe and in good health. But instead of sharing in the joy, Ronald became angry and refused to enter the house to join the celebration.

Ronald kept a record of his brother's wasteful actions, comparing himself to the brother he now viewed as heartless. *"My father has never made merry for me,"* he thought. *"He never gave me a goat to celebrate, nor any substance to show his favor."* He felt his own good behavior had been overlooked, and his brother, who had squandered everything, was now being lavished with attention. Ronald's bitterness grew; he could not understand why his brother, who had been so reckless, was being treated with such kindness. Perhaps he would have preferred if his brother never returned, rather than seeing him *"bounce back"* and receive such forgiveness.

He could not accept how his father had received his brother; not only restored physically, but also in his right mind, having repented of his vices. This thought offended

Ronald deeply and fueled his anger. He showed his resentment by refusing to join the celebration, rejecting the opportunity to share in the father's joy.

The eldest son boasted of his own virtue and obedience, yet he failed to recognize the change in his brother's heart. He approached his father with a complaint, saying, *"All these years, I have faithfully served you and have never disobeyed your commands. Yet, it is your wayward son who brought you shame, not me. In other words, it should be me that you celebrate."*

In his words, there was a spirit of self-entitlement. *"You have never given me a kid, that I might make merry with my friends,"* he added. Jealousy stirred within him as he counted the wrongs his brother had committed, yet failed to see his own pride. If he had desired a celebration, his father would have been more than willing to grant it, but instead, he resented the lavish feast his father had prepared for his brother. The eldest son, Ronald, was ill-mannered both toward his father and his brother. He refused to join in the celebration, thinking that the same house should not be shared by him and his runaway brother. No, not in his father's house.

When he saw that his father had welcomed his lost brother back, Ronald stood off, unable to bring himself to greet him. He could not find it in his heart to accept the forgiveness and grace that God, like a father, had extended to the son who had returned. Even worse, he refused to acknowledge Raymond as his brother, saying, *"This son of yours,"* which sounded both arrogant and disrespectful toward his father. Ronald accused, *"He is your son who wasted your wealth on harlots,"* showing dishonor and resentment toward the kindness his father had shown Raymond. And he repeatedly complained, *"You have killed the fatted calf for him."*

Ronald's confusion was evident. He failed to remember that the fatted calf belonged to the father, who had the right to use it as he pleased. It was the father's decision to celebrate his son's safe return, and for Ronald to cast blame at that moment was unacceptable. The eldest son had completely forgotten his place as a son, not as a father. He had no reasonable grounds for complaint. Instead of joining the celebration, he chose to nitpick, begrudging the fact that Raymond was being treated to a feast, clothed as a prince, and given all he needed.

Home Sweet Home

One can only imagine the deep feelings Raymond must have experienced in that moment. As he sat at the table, nourished and celebrated, he reflected on the days of famine and hardship he had endured. Meanwhile, his brother was preoccupied with petty grievances that could have been easily let go. But no, Ronald chose to hold onto every small argument as if it were a prized entitlement. Even though Raymond knew he had done wrong and had received his father's forgiveness, he also understood that Ronald needed to find forgiveness in his own heart. Perhaps Raymond should reach out to his brother, reminding him that forgiveness was the true path to peace, not continued bitterness.

Ronald refused to join the celebration because he was burdened with hatred, resentment, pride, and arrogance. Envy had taken root in his heart, poisoning his thoughts against both his father and his brother. He could not accept that his father had welcomed his wayward brother back with such grace. Ronald failed to realize that harboring jealousy would only corrode him from within, like cancer in the bones, eating away at his peace. His attitude was in dire need of repentance and healing.

Ronald's heart was filled with indifference and complaints, which was especially troubling given that, as the elder son, he should have known better and acted with wisdom in such a critical moment. God, in His wisdom, addresses us individually, not as part of the crowd. Even though Ronald refused to join in the celebration of his brother's safe return, his father didn't react harshly. Instead, he went out to him with a gentle rebuke.

The father could have simply said, *"If Ronald won't celebrate his brother's return, then let him stay outside,"* but instead he asked, *"Isn't this house mine, to welcome my son as I please?"* The father, full of understanding and love, extended grace even to his elder son, who needed healing in his heart.

The father didn't feel obligated to explain the depth of forgiveness; how it reaches deep into the core of unforgiveness and transforms past wrongs into nothingness, fit only for the trash bin. He could have reminded Ronald of how many times he should forgive his brother. Instead, he simply encouraged him to reflect on the example of forgiveness Jesus gave. *"Remember, son,"* the father said, *"how Jesus asked His Father, 'Forgive the people who have wronged me, for they know not what they do.'"* This was the kind of forgiveness Ronald needed to understand, not just for his brother, but for himself.

Meanwhile, Raymond was welcomed home with warmth and joy. The father had prepared a place for him, offering clean clothes, shoes for his feet, a ring on his finger, and a feast to celebrate his return. Raymond had successfully bounced back from the edge, and his father's grace and love were the foundation of his restoration.

RAYMOND'S PRAYER

Though I've wandered from my father's house, I thank You for making my return possible. I come before You with a heart full of gratitude for Your mercy and grace. Lord, I ask for Your peace to fill my mind, calming any anxieties or worries. Please give me the serenity to handle the unexpected challenges that may arise and threaten to disrupt the vision You have for my life. I trust in Your peace, knowing that through You, all things are made possible. In Jesus' name, I pray.

Father, I ask that You help Ronald repent of his wrong attitude and indifference towards myself. May he accept Your healing and the opportunity to love again. Lord we both need Your presence every hour, for only by Your grace can the power of tempers be defeated. As we look to You, our Guide and Stay, may we be kept through every storm and sunshine. "O Lord, abide with me!"

Father, I also ask for wisdom to celebrate the achievements of others with a pure heart. Help me to honor time as the precious gift it is, used according to Your will, never taken for granted. I acknowledge that time cannot be reversed, and I trust that my moments are in Your hands. I leave them there, knowing You will guide me.

Please enable me to share each moment meaningfully with others, caring for them and telling the story of how Your love is rich in mercy and grace. May I be a reflection of Your goodness in every relationship and interaction.

In the name of Jesus Christ, Your Son, I pray. Amen.

Chapter 12

LIVING IN HARMONY

It is vitally important for families to live together in harmony, especially after a major disturbance among family members, such as recovering from sickness, a runaway child, time spent in prison, or other significant upheavals. During these times, healing and deliverance are crucial for the individuals involved. If not addressed properly, these disruptions can quickly escalate, creating a crisis that affects the entire family. Tension, blame, and unresolved conflict can tear at the fabric of the family unit, making it vital to foster understanding, compassion, and patience.

Everyone has expectations of others, parents hope their children will grow up to be responsible citizens, friends expect loyalty, and employers anticipate faithfulness and honesty from their workers. Timekeeping and harmony in the workplace are often seen as essential to success. However, when those expectations are unmet, whether due to personal failure or external circumstances, they can create obstacles. Life is a constant process of giving and taking, and it often unfolds in ways that go beyond our expectations.

Times of failure can become hindrances, but they also offer opportunities for growth and learning. Life teaches us that setbacks are inevitable, and how we handle them often shapes our future. The key is to approach failure with a spirit of understanding, knowing that no one is perfect. By doing so, we create space for healing, forgiveness, and ultimately, the restoration of peace within our families and relationships.

In times of crisis, family members must be willing to give and take, learn from each other and extend grace. It is through this process that families rebuild and emerge stronger. The way a family responds to challenges defines not just the individuals involved, but the family as a whole, shaping its future for years to come.

Here lies the first proof of the problem: Raymond left home and made a mess of his life. When he found himself at his wits' end, he decided to return home. Thank God he didn't return in a coffin, laid to rest in the grave. He came home alive, with no need for burial arrangements. No, he returned home safe and sound. He had never been been incarcerated since he left home; his father's prayers had kept him alive, escaping the lion's mouth over the many years he lived on the edge. *"My son is alive and well!"*

As parents, this was an exceptional occasion for family celebration and thanksgiving, perhaps even bringing the entire community together to celebrate the return of the son who was once lost but has now come home safe and sound. In most family situations, when such a moment occurs, differences are set aside, and everyone joins in the celebration, blending their emotions and joy in the process.

While this situation may not have happened to you personally, it has undoubtedly happened to someone in your family. As a result, you are inevitably involved because of the family bloodline, which is of utmost importance.

The older son, Ronald, might have feared that his father would ask him to share his remaining inheritance with his brother. He complained bitterly, *"It's not fair. I'll probably have nothing left. What if I want to get married and start a family? I wouldn't have the chance, all because of my irresponsible brother, who thinks he can waste his inheritance and come back home completely broke."* Though it was meant to be a time of harmony in the father's house, a sense of misgiving still darkened the atmosphere.

There was conflict in the home due to the older brother's unforgiving attitude toward his sibling. He grumbled, *"This boy didn't even bother to check if my father and I were alive or dead, and now he comes bouncing back, calling it a return 'from the edge.' It's not fair. No one pushed him into danger; whatever 'the edge' means, he went off the rails on his own and nearly went over."*

Raymond knew his brother had every right to remind him of his mistakes and failures, so he remained silent, as humble as a calf. He thought to himself, *"If my brother knew what kind of work I was doing, feeding pigs, he would probably disown me. Feeding pigs?"*

Raymond felt the full force of his brother's anger and turned to God in prayer. *"Lord, I come to you with all my heart. Jesus, forgive me for causing so much pain to my family. Make me whole again. If you do this for me, I will follow you all the days of my life."*

Raymond made it a point to pray at every opportunity. He simply could not keep from expressing his gratitude to God for bringing him safely back to his father's house.

It was as though gratitude was overflowing from within him, and it was evident that he had truly changed. He no longer held back what was due for the wasted days of wandering. His father noticed this change, saw him praying, and felt hopeful that his son was now on the right path.

Raymond had read in 1 Peter: 5 about casting his cares on Jesus. He thought to himself, *"That sounds good, but for me, there are too many challenges, wrongs, and disappointments. It's too much to carry, especially dealing with my brother's attitude toward me. I'm tired."* He cried, *"Help me,"* but not loud enough for his father to hear. *"Give me the strength to overcome these terrible, wearisome challenges."*

Raymond prayed, *"Lord, rebuke me not in Your hot wrath, neither chasten me in Your displeasure. For Your arrows stick fast in me, and Your hand presses me sore."*

"There is no soundness in my flesh because of Your anger; neither is there any rest in my bones because of my sin. My iniquities have gone over my head; as a heavy burden, they

are too heavy for me. Lord, I am bowed down greatly; I go mourning all the day. All my desire is before You, and my groaning is not hidden from You. My heart pants; my strength fails me. As for the light of my eyes, it also is gone from me. My lovers and friends stand aloof from my sore, and my kinsmen stand afar off. For in You, O Lord, I hope you will hear, Lord, hear me, for I am ready to halt, and my sorrow is continually before You. Forsake me not Lord, O my God, do not be far from me. Make haste to help me, O Lord, the God of my salvation."

Raymond's brother Ronald saw him praying and was taken aback. He asked in disbelief, *"Is this real? Has this wayward boy really remembered how to pray? How can he just start praying again without being chastened for all his wrongdoings? It's not fair. I've never done anything as wicked and selfish as he did, and yet he seems to get away with it."*

Although his father's strict discipline was meant to guide them in the right way, now that Raymond had returned home, he was trying to make amends both with our father and with God. *"What's going on here?"* Ronald moaned. *"I'll have a private talk with Father about his son's behavior—praying as if he were without faults—while I'm treated like the bad son who ran away, squandered everything, and now just bounces back to be celebrated."*

Ronald felt heartbroken and quietly confessed, *"My younger brother prayed with such confidence. It seems he had faith, not fear, and wasn't afraid to express himself before our father and before God."*

He then began to question his own actions, wondering if he had been too harsh. *"Perhaps I should not demand perfection for Raymond's mistakes, since I am not without fault and also in need of forgiveness,"* he reflected. He considered asking Raymond how he had found such peace, but wasn't sure if it was the right time. Maybe he should wait a little longer to see if the moment and the celebration of Raymond's return, would fade away like a fleeting dream.

Ronald considered deeply and then said, *"I've read in the Bible that it is good and pleasant for brethren to dwell together in unity, and that unity is a beautiful thing. Oh, how much I need that peace; the peace I see in my brother. Even though I have no idea what he's been through since he left home, or the depth of what he experienced to bounce back from the edge, it couldn't have been easy. But by the look of things and the lengths my father went to in rescuing him, I see a story unfolding."*

"I would like to be a part of that story," he added softly.

"First and foremost, how my father forgave Raymond for what he has done is a mystery. How could he forgive after all that Raymond put him through? I will never truly know." He paused, reflecting. *"Now that Raymond has returned home, my father can finally unburden himself from the heavy load he'd been carrying for so long—getting up at the crack of dawn, praying, and pleading with God for his son's safety. And now, through God's help, he's come home safely. His life has certainly been transformed; he seems better than when he left home to wander in the fields of sin."*

"My brother's attitude toward me seems to have changed," Ronald reflected. *"His rebellious behavior has now turned into a respectful attitude toward our father and me, which has always been due to both of us. It seems as though he has learned some honorable lessons while he was away from home."*

The father, upon hearing his eldest son speak, responded with confidence, speaking of the power of prayer. *"I just want to thank God and everyone who interceded for Raymond. He came home a changed person, with the right attitude. I personally believe in the power of prayer that went up into heaven. I believe the Holy Spirit came down and worked with Raymond. I prayed, and now I am at peace, knowing that God will do what He promised. Right now, to Him be all the praise, honor, and glory."*

The father then reflected, *"Now that my sons are together, I want to enlighten them about the importance of forgiveness and the danger of unforgiveness."* He asked, *"Do you ever feel guilty about an issue that you may not be able to forgive someone for? Though wrong thoughts aren't what you really want to dwell on, even if they seem harmless, they can become toxic. If left unchecked, even a thought can become emotionally or spiritually dangerous."*

The father continued, *"Each thought you have is measurable and occupies mental space. Thoughts are active—they grow and change. Your thoughts will influence every decision, word, action, and physical reaction you make. Every time you think about something, it actually makes changes in your brain and body, for better or for worse. When an individual refuses to forgive others, it is crucial to ask God for help in setting you free from the spirit of unforgiveness."*

Scolding, as a father, I could have chosen not to forgive my son and others for their unseasonable and disrespectful behavior, but instead, I chose to let it go by taking positive actions that free both myself and others. Words from the father: *"My beloved boys, from this day on, I pray that you will watch your thoughts, for something as small as a minor irritation can become toxic if left unchecked. These thoughts need to be swept away."*

Be careful with every thought. Whatever is good, right, and lovely, think on these things. Always think good thoughts of each other, no matter how difficult or gruesome a situation may seem. There is good in every thought when unraveled. The best will emerge because God has designed you with hope and He has shown the best way to overcome the most difficult experiences. This is not about how the brain functions, but about the grace God provides.

As a loving and considerate father, I thought it important to regularly remind my two sons of the importance of finding wisdom. Don't be wise in your own thinking; instead, examine your attitude toward each other. Raymond has been to the edge and almost fallen over, but for the mercies of God and through prayer, he recovered and is here to tell his story. Otherwise, he would not be sitting here today. He managed to bounce back from the edge with his mind restored.

Therefore, you have a duty to encourage one another, offering hope to those in need, supporting and establishing each other. Never be drawn back to the edge of any circumstance. Though you may encounter temptations, you must stand firm in what you believe and not be led astray by your own impulses.

FASELY ACCUSED

....

There are countless individuals behind bars, falsely accused of crimes they did not commit. Many are subjected to penalties for minor offenses, enduring rough treatment and being locked away in prison as part of a legal punishment. Some never live long enough to clear their names, while others suffer untimely demises in custody, with no voice to advocate for their innocence.

Young Jimmy, sold into servitude to a high-ranking officer with connections to public figures and business, was greatly blessed despite his circumstances. Even in the house of his servitude, God prospered him. His brothers stripped him of his multicolored coat, but they could not take away his virtue or his prudence. Though separated from his brothers and banished from his father's house, he was never abandoned by his God.

His master, recognizing his integrity, eventually made him steward of his household. However, his master's wife, overcome by temptation, sought to scandalize her behavior in Jimmy's presence, attempting to satisfy her desires. Her sin began with a look. She cast her eyes upon him, shameless and daring in her pursuit. She imagined herself in an illicit affair with this handsome, strong, and intelligent young man, seeing him as an object to fulfill her burning desires. Perhaps her husband was not satisfying her, but Jimmy, younger and stronger, caught her fancy.

Jimmy's greatest temptation was not from an external enemy, but from his mistress; a woman of high status whom he was bound to obey. Her favor could significantly advance his position, and to slight her would risk making an enemy of someone powerful. The temptation was within his very household, where he had to navigate his business with discretion. His mistress's advances placed him in a precarious position, where rejecting her could cost him dearly. If he was accused, he could not deny the crime.

Despite her persistent attempts to corrupt him, Jimmy remained steadfast in his refusal. However, she sought revenge for his virtue by falsely accusing him of attempting to make advances on her. She told her husband, who immediately believed the accusation, and there was no remedy for Jimmy. His fate was sealed, he would be imprisoned, locked away among the king's prisoners.

Her husband, though he knew of Jimmy's character, chose to punish him severely. Fearing disobedience to his wife, he condemned Jimmy to the worst prison, far from any friends or supporters. But even in this dire situation, the Lord was with Jimmy, showing him mercy. No gates or bars could keep God's presence from His faithful servant.

The king, though aware of Jimmy's innocence, could not release him without angering his wife. So, Jimmy remained in prison, yet God's hand was upon him. During his time in the king's prison, he met a butler and a baker, both of whom were also incarcerated. One of them, recognizing Jimmy's innocence, befriended him. Through their conversations, they learned that Jimmy had the ability to interpret dreams, a gift that would soon play a pivotal role in his journey.

One night, the chief baker had a troubling dream and shared it with Jimmy. The interpretation of the dream saddened him deeply. Jimmy, noticing the baker's distress, inquired about the cause of his sorrow. The baker, feeling the weight of his dream's meaning, asked Jimmy to interpret it. While Jimmy knew that only God has the power to reveal the true meaning of dreams. He sometimes bestows this gift on certain individuals, as He chooses. The baker insisted, urging Jimmy to share the interpretation.

Jimmy remained clear and truthful in his response. Despite the injustice he had faced—being sold by his brothers, wrongfully imprisoned by his mistress, and judged by his master, he chose not to harbor bitterness. In that moment, he reflected the wisdom that when seeking to defend oneself, it is crucial to avoid speaking ill of others. Vindication comes not through blaming or upbraiding others, but by proving one's own innocence with integrity. In other words, Jimmy understood the importance of leaving the judgment in God's hands.

The interpretations of the chief butler and baker's dreams came to pass: one was restored to his office, while the other was hanged. The butler was overjoyed when he learned that the interpretation of his dream favored him. Before leaving, Jimmy asked him to remember him to the king, to speak on his behalf as an innocent man in need of a fair hearing. Unfortunately, the butler forgot, but Jimmy did not become discouraged. He did not complain about his situation or the false accusations against him. Instead, he continued to pray with hope, trusting that one day God would free him from the prison and restore his life.

Jimmy pondered many ways to escape his unjust circumstances, but every attempt failed. Despite his hardships, he never considered giving up or ending his life. He refused to lose hope and maintained a positive outlook, believing that one day he would bounce back to his rightful place. In the meantime, he made the most of every opportunity to pray, holding onto his faith in God. The prison may have confined his body, but it could not imprison his spirit. His mind and soul remained strong, rooted in the trust he had in God, the only true God of his father.

His cellmates heard him praying and saw his unwavering faith. They knew Jimmy was a good man who deserved a chance to be set free. Yet, despite his goodness, people often fail to celebrate the virtues they see in others, instead choosing to focus on their flaws, real or imagined, to craft a narrative that suits their needs. But God sees all.

One of Jimmy's cellmates, Tommy, was eventually released. Jimmy asked him to remember him when he was free and to mention his name to the governor. Unfortunately, Tommy forgot, and Jimmy's name was never brought before the authorities for consideration.

However, Jimmy never allowed bitterness or a bad attitude to dominate his thoughts because of Tommy's failure to mention him. Instead, he continued to pray with firm belief that his time for release would come. And eventually, it did. Jimmy was delivered from prison, and how joyful he was when he walked out, free at last, bouncing back to the life he deserved.

The takeaway from Jimmy's story is clear: never give up, for your time will come, no matter how long it takes. Being forgiven means having a debt of sin paid off without having to repay it. Consider this, when you must take time off work to care for a loved one, your financial burdens can quickly pile up. Similarly, there are innocent people all over the world who are caught in the web of false accusations and unfairly punished for crimes they never committed. Some hire lawyers to plead their cases, but they still face unjust sentences, with nothing changing.

Can you imagine being in such a dilemma? What if no one believed your truth, and only lies were trusted? Who would plead your case?

Though evil was plotted against Jimmy, and a mischievous scheme was devised to bring him down, they were ultimately unable to carry it out. Jimmy was vindicated in the name of the Lord. It is vital to be mindful of your character and set strong boundaries around it. Be diligent in who you trust and associate with. Many people will try to sabotage your progress, and some will even go to great lengths to have you wrongfully imprisoned. However, as long as you are under the protection of the all-seeing eye of God, you are safe.

Chapter 13

ABUNDANTLY LIVING

Many people seek an abundance of material things such as money, weapons, or riches, yet these only provide temporary satisfaction. True fulfillment comes from living in the abundance of God's spiritual blessings, such as goodness, pardon, peace, truth, answered prayers, grace, and mercy. These are the keys to happiness. When we live in the abundance of God's goodness, His nature is revealed to us, He is merciful, gracious, longsuffering, and abundant in goodness and truth. A person who chooses to live according to these attributes will experience true abundance and receive pardon for their sins.

These blessings can be obtained by putting away sin and following God's commandments. As Scripture says, *"Let the wicked forsake his ways, and the unrighteous man his thoughts, and return to the Lord, and He will abundantly pardon and grant peace."* Turning away from the edge of sin provides insight and foresight, even in these dark times filled with atrocities. Those who forsake God and reject His ways have no true hope; but for those who seek Him, hope is steadfast and sure. Hope is not just optimism; it's the confident expectation that better days are ahead, even when things seem bleak.

Why do we need hope? Hope generates a lively and promising future, one that is brighter than the present. When we reflect on our lives, we should forget the past and press forward to the future. Staying stuck in past regrets will only lead to more pain and questions. There is no reason to live in a lack of hope, joy, or peace. Instead, embrace the exchange of a life of freedom that is offered through Jesus. He is calling you to a life of abundance and a greater future.

God has placed great value on you because you seized the opportunity to bounce back from the edge of no return. Your mistakes, no matter how big, are not greater than God's amazing forgiveness and grace. Therefore, seek His forgiveness, live in its abundance, and build your life on the assurance of Jesus' teachings and commands. Be committed to His way of life, and willingly follow His path. Choosing to live a bountiful life after coming back from the edge is a tremendous and rewarding endeavor. Living authentically, with nothing to hide and embracing transparency, will give you confidence when sharing your story of recovery, of where you were and where you are now.

To stay on this path, seek positive activities that will keep your mind engaged, such as thinking, reading, and meditating on God's Word. Keep away from negativity, and move away from past hurts and shame. Instead, seek God's approval, as He assures you, *"You are safe in My hands."*

Though Raymond was weak in body, soul, and spirit, and nearly went over the edge, he chose to speak words of affirmation and courage to himself. He intentionally bounced back from tthe edge and when the opportunity arose to encourage someone else, he took it. You never know what someone has been through, whether they lived in a mansion or a pigpen.

We must refrain from making the same mistakes over and over. Change happens gradually, and though it's never easy, it's always possible. Acknowledge every step of progress along the way; your experience will help others understand and accept you, rather than speaking aimlessly.

While facing his struggles, Raymond didn't let anger take hold. He understood that prolonged anger only diminishes joy, elevates toxic chemicals in the body, and raises blood pressure. Everyone will become upset or angry at times, it's a natural human response. Instead of focusing on petty grievances, why not use those moments to encourage others, recognizing the cause of their hurt, rather than attacking them? Do all you can to address the root of the hurt, request help when needed, and remember that life is not about entitlement, but about compassion and growth.

The secret to poise in the midst of trouble is faith, not in yourself, nor in friends, possessions, or circumstances, but in God. Your sense of assurance and stability grows from the firm conviction that God can and will control the situation, using it to fulfill His purpose. One way to enjoy an abundant life after bouncing back from the edge is to welcome those who approach you with heartfelt compliments about your persistence in moving from a downtrodden path to a life rich in positive awareness and fullness. You can use the same energy to encourage others, offering praise and recognition when they deserve it. For example, the man who continues helping others, even with little appreciation, does so because he aims to please God and those around him.

Abundantly Living

As you journey through life, you will encounter many individuals who are burdened by mistakes, failures, disappointments, and grief. Their hearts are filled with discouragement, unable to reflect on the beauty of the world with all its contrasts: joy and sorrow and sorrow, thorns and roses. It is unwise to focus solely on past wounds and disappointments, mourning over them until you become overwhelmed with discouragement.

A discouraged soul is filled with darkness, having shut out the light and casting shadows on the paths of others. You hold the very Word of God in your hands, knowing His saving grace and the comfort of His Spirit. Yet, even with this knowledge, you may still ask, "Why me, Lord?" when faced with hardships.

In summary, there is no room for negativity when God's hand is upon your life. Every difficult situation is filtered through His perfect love. You will never suffer more than what is necessary. Yes, there are deep waters you must wade through, and fiery darts that test your character. But in the midst of them, God promises to be your partner, a companion, and a faithful friend. As Romans 5:10 reminds us, He will perfect, establish, strengthen, and settle you through it all.

PROGRESSIVE ATTITUDE

....

The positive steps you have taken to move away from the edge must be maintained throughout your life to prevent something worse: falling back into the consequences you've left behind. Strive for progress, not just any progress, but real, positive progress that demands your full commitment. Do not stand still after bouncing back from the edge of idleness, doing nothing.

Always remember the passion you had for positive change, even when all seemed lost, when you couldn't see whether you would survive or be buried, like someone whose life had come to an end. It's possible that some who return from the edge may not bounce back on their own but are helped by others because they couldn't rise by themselves. Some individuals may have given up just before their deliverance, right before the dawn of their awaited victory. If only they had held on a little longer, they would have experienced the joy of triumph.

God forbid that this would be your story. Remember the parable of the prodigal son who asked his father for his inheritance and left home with no desire to improve or invest in his future, only to waste time in unlawful and fleeting pleasures. The key is making progress, moving rapidly toward your goal with anticipation and purpose. While making progress, you should aim for change and improvement, working toward a better version of yourself, rather than staying stagnant.

Some individuals may resist leaving the mentality that got them to the edge in the first place. They prefer to stay stuck, lying down in despair, complaining about their lack of help. But true progress begins with a change of mindset, gradually developing stability in stages. Start by cultivating a positive state of mind, where your thoughts are measured and deliberate. A progressive thinker focuses on thoughts that are true, lovely, pure, and of good report. By working on these daily, you will make steady progress, looking to Jesus, the Author and Finisher of your faith, for guidance.

When you decide to move forward, to advance, and make progress, you cannot remain idle, lying down, or sleeping until all hours while merely thinking of moving forward. Just like a stream of water, once it finds its path, it will naturally flow downstream until it reaches a wider river. Similarly, when you choose to turn from negative ways and walk the right path, even in a desert, you will find a stream that will quench your thirst and satisfy you. The emptiness of your soul will be filled, and your spiritual hunger will be satisfied as you seek more of God.

A simple rule is this: What does not move up or forward will go down or backward. This is especially true in the spiritual realm. God intends for your spiritual development to be continuous, not a cycle of starting and stopping. You must avoid becoming overwhelmed in your thoughts and actions. Sometimes, progress requires a push, like a woman in labor, whose desire to give birth becomes a life-and-death situation. The child must be delivered within a certain time frame, or medical intervention will be necessary.

This analogy does not imply that you will never encounter hardship, disappointment, or failure. Rather, it reminds you that trusting in God does not eliminate life's challenges, but it empowers you to find strength in your weakness, victory in your failures, and the divine ability to rise above your problems, all while making progress through Him who loves you.

An important part of progress is finding joy in serving God and getting involved in causes of truth and justice. Share what you have discovered to help those who are oppressed, neglected, or exploited. Befriend the lonely, comfort the brokenhearted, show love and concern for minority groups, and obey the laws of the land. Developing a meaningful purpose in life, one that brings unity, direction, and harmony, will fill you with life, not despair.

Make progress in even the small things that may seem insignificant at the moment. These little steps will accumulate, and over time, they will help you fulfill God's highest purpose for your life. Avoid pursuing unspiritual goals such as mere pleasure, wealth, and prestige—those things that are self-serving. Instead, focus on personal goals that align with your values and God's will. Reflect on what you want to achieve in the coming years. Even when you're on your deathbed, looking back at your life, what do you want to have accomplished?

When you were at the edge, it seemed as though nothing positive could be hoped for. But now that you've bounced back, it's a great opportunity to make the most of today, doing things you were once unable to do, making sense of the situation. However, instead of moving forward and making progress, many people's lives remain aimless. Others may have the right intentions but fail to take action towards their goals.

In the journey of life, one significant enemy is doubt, which can manifest in many ways, affecting your health, social status, job, or family. Intellectual doubts can also undermine your confidence in the Word of God, shaking your spiritual stability and robbing you of joy and effectiveness in service.

When troubles pile up and prayers seem unanswered, it's natural to wonder if you've been abandoned. In those moments, remember the reassurance in God's Word: "Can a woman forget her nursing child, and have no compassion on the child of her womb? Even though some may forget, I will never forget you." God's love and faithfulness are unwavering, even when it feels like the world has turned away.

One common irritant that fuels doubt is the fear of change. Prayer is a powerful antidote to doubt. With a strong conviction in eternal values and the knowledge that God's help is always available, we need not doubt His ability or willingness to meet our needs. The same power that parted the Red Sea for His people is still at work today, ready to open paths for us in our time of need.

On a practical level, changing our attitudes towards the poor and the elderly is part of making progress. It's not too much to ask to show kindness and lend a helping hand to those less fortunate. Every person has a place in this remarkable world, and those who are well-off should help those in need until they are in a better position to help themselves.

As for the elderly, they had their time of youthfulness, and we must not forget to care for and assist them with a favorable attitude. While it may be harder for older individuals to bounce back from difficult circumstances, they still have value. Some may need to take it slowly, and others may require the support of others, but getting back on their feet, even in broken pieces, is still a victory.

When you return from the edge of difficult circumstances, where negative thoughts seem to dominate, it can feel as if nothing is possible. Yet, in the midst of it all, you hold on to the belief that one day you will bounce back. For instance, you might declare, *"I will not go under."* You may recover from temptation and the snare of giving in, but others who have been swayed by your influence may not be able to bounce back. This is why it's so important to speak only words that bring spiritual strength and life.

I have not gone over the edge, by the grace of God. I'm here today, living to share my experience with those I encounter. It is possible to walk or bounce back from the enticement of negative influences or bad company, people who may have wished for your downfall. God has a purpose for each life, leading to real adventure for those willing to cooperate with Him. He can use extraordinary means to fulfill His plan, often when you least expect it.

As the Bible says: *"Do not count yourself as if you have already attained, but do one thing: forgetting the things that are behind, and reaching forward to those things which are ahead, pressing towards the goal for the prize of the upward call of God in Christ."* Keep your mind and heart focused on your God-given goals. Tell yourself, "It is possible. All possibilities for success are within my reach." You have paid the price of humility, and nothing should hold you back from progressing, except for yourself.

The good news is that forgiveness and eternal life are gifts from God's grace, received through faith in Christ and available to all people. Obedience flows from a relationship with God, but it will never create or earn that relationship. Hope is like the silver beam of sunlight breaking through a storm-darkened sky. It is comfort in times of hardship, a letter from far away, the first spring bird perched on a snow-covered twig and the finish line coming into view. Hope is a rainbow, a loving touch and above all, knowing God and resting in His love.

PRAY

I thank You for Your help and take the initiative to make progress in gaining a divine perspective as I move forward. Father God, I will not waste the pain I've experienced on trivial things, but I will strive to progress to the next level in You, O Lord.

According to Your promises, Father, if I abide in Your Word and Your Word abides in me, You will be my Father. I ask You in the name of Your Son, Jesus Christ, to give me the strength and steadfastness to let Your Word dwell in me.

Lord, please help me not to remember the sins of my youth, nor allow them to keep me in slavery. Help me to embrace Your freedom through the sacrifice of Your Son, Jesus Christ.

Remember Your tender mercies and loving-kindness, for they have been from of old. Thank You, Lord, for all the blessings and favor You have declared over me. I give You all the praise in Jesus' precious name. Amen.

BOUNCING BACK FROM THE EDGE

Chapter *14*

SPIRITUAL SUSTENANCE

At this critical junction, as we move away from the edge, it is essential to acquire spiritual sustenance. The true measure of what sustains life can only come from God, the giver of life. God has always provided sustenance for those who fear Him. For instance, when His prophet Elijah was in desperate need of food and water in the wilderness, God provided. He gave Elijah water from a brook and sent ravens to bring him food twice a day. The ravens, unlikely carriers of provision, were God's chosen instruments, showing that God's provision does not depend on ordinary means. When the brook dried up, God directed Elijah to the Jordan River, a fresh source of water, demonstrating that God's provisions are limitless and not bound to any particular source.

"It is God only and no other god."

Spiritual sustenance also comes from God's security over His people. He protects believers throughout the journey of salvation. The Bible teaches that salvation is not earned by human effort. God is the author of salvation, and it is He who guarantees its completion. Salvation does not depend on church attendance, good works, reading scriptures, or penance. It is Christ alone who protects and keeps believers. We do not have the strength to secure ourselves; it is only by God's grace that we are kept.

In order to maintain our spiritual sustenance, we must continually refresh and rejuvenate ourselves in the Word of God, making it a daily practice. It is through God's Word that we are sustained and strengthened for the journey ahead.

INDULGING IN THE WORD

....

There are many spiritual practices that are essential for sustaining you spiritually. For instance, the Word of God, prayer, praise, and fasting are powerful, nourishing

Spiritual Sustenance

practices that provide lasting spiritual sustenance for body, soul, and spirit. These practices are in abundant supply and never run out, much like a river that flows continually, day and night, year-round.

In order to maintain a balanced spiritual diet, it's important to function on all cylinders every day. Those who God deals with must do so with trust. Jesus teaches us, *"Seek first the kingdom of God and His righteousness, and all these things will be added to you."* The Word of God is your primary source of spiritual sustenance. It reveals who God is, what He has done, and what He will do.

After bouncing back from the edge, hide the Word of God in your heart and meditate on it day and night. The Word will protect you from the temptation to return to the edge of negativity or sin. Continually seek the Word for guidance, learning, and understanding.

The Word of God is living and powerful. It is sharper than any two-edged sword, piercing even to the division of soul and spirit, and discerning the thoughts and intents of the heart (Hebrews 4:12).

It is also called the *'Word of life.'* As Philippians 2:16 says, *"Holding fast the Word of life, so that I may rejoice in the day of Christ, that I have not run in vain or labored in vain."* The Word of God is a lamp to your feet and a light to your path, guiding you and giving direction to where you are going.

SUSTENANCE THROUGH PRAYER

Dear God, I give You thanks for Your help, and I commit to taking the initiative in making progress by gaining a divine perspective as I move forward. Father God, I will not waste the pain I've experienced on trivial matters, but I will make progress to the next level in You, O Lord.

Father, according to Your promises, if I abide in Your Word and Your Word abides in me, You will be my Father. I ask You, in the name of Your Son, Jesus Christ, to give me the strength and steadfastness to let Your Word abide in me. Lord, please help me not to dwell on the sins of my youth, nor allow them to keep me in slavery, but to accept Your freedom in the name of Jesus Christ.

Lord, remember Your tender mercies and loving-kindness, for they have been from of old. Thank You, Lord, for all the blessings and favor You have declared over me. I give You thanks in Jesus' precious name. Amen.

SUSTENANCE THROUGH PRAYER

To maintain spiritual sustenance, prayer is an effectual strategy. Prayer is a petition to God, like one making a request before a judge. Although prayer times may sometimes feel cold, listless, or difficult, especially if the heart isn't already aflame with spiritual fervour. The atmosphere of prayer should ignite and set your heart ablaze, fueling progress toward the greater things God has in store for you.

In your prayers, it's essential to thank God for His past favors. You owe Him a debt of gratitude, which you can discharge through praise and worship. As far as you are concerned, expect greater things from God in both the present and the future, remembering that what He has done in the past is still possible in the future.

There are various kinds of prayer for different situations, but they all come down to praying effectively to God in the name of Jesus. This includes making supplications on behalf of others, interceding for families, nations, and people far and near. Prayer is powerful, special, and effective, especially when prayed in faith. The Bible tells us that prayers offered in faith are mighty, able to pull down strongholds.

The practice of praying without ceasing will elevate you to a deeper relationship with God, turning you into a first-class citizen in Christ. Prayer helps you see what God wants you to notice. It provides you with a *"God-eye view,"* enhancing your awareness and giving you a heightened sense to perceive spiritual realities. The more you pray, the more you notice; the less you pray, the less you perceive. Therefore, devote yourself to prayer, being watchful and thankful, as Paul instructs in Colossians 4:2.

Fervent prayer gives direction to your progress. It will empower you to desire greatness and go further than you expect. Prayer clears the path, providing a clear vision of where you are headed. Prayer is not a luxury—it is a lifelong commitment to give of yourself to God. It involves a mutual exchange, where you don't just say *"Give me, Lord"* as if it's a one-way street. Prayer is a holistic process of offering yourself and receiving from God.

Spiritual Sustenance

Prayer grants power and insight, helping you progress even in dark times, without doubt or fear. As you bounce back from the edge, develop your prayer life in these areas. These prayer habits will keep you grounded, stabilized and focused on progressing forward. Spend more time in prayer around the throne of grace, where grace is given based on your immediate need. God will not give you tomorrow's grace today; He provides fresh grace each new day, meeting your needs as they arise.

The Holy Spirit, as your lawyer, pleads on your behalf before God. This is a reminder that you should never come before God in prayer only for yourself, but also for others. When you pray, say, *"Give us this day our daily bread,"* recognizing that your Father in heaven, the source of all resources, is the supplier for the entire community. The Father owns everything, and when you face hardships such as losing a job, He provides all your needs according to His riches in glory by Christ Jesus. His house is a house of prayer, a place where your petitions are heard.

To petition in prayer, you need an understanding of spiritual ownership; an awareness that, as citizens of God's kingdom, you have legal rights to approach Him and expect answers. However, if you are not born again, you do not have the constitutional right to make demands of the

Governor of the Kingdom. Only through salvation can you claim your rights in the Kingdom of God.

The kindness of God, for which He is to be praised, is evident in all that He has done for us. As the Scripture says, *"Surely they are My people, children who will be true to Me, and so He became their Savior"* (Isaiah 63:7). The loving-kindness of the Lord is shown in the multitude of His mercies toward Israel and toward us.

As Isaiah 63:7 further explains, *"I shall make mention of the loving-kindness of the Lord, according to all that the Lord has granted you, and the greatness of His goodness toward the house of Israel, which He has granted them, according to the multitude of His loving-kindness."* The goodness of God is evident in all that He has bestowed upon you, relating to life, godliness, and every blessing for you and your family. It is imperative that you bless God for the mercies He has granted both you and others.

Remember, God's goodness is not based on your merits but on His mercies and loving-kindness. Everything you have received comes from His grace, not your works.

To improve your personal potential and progress in prayer, especially after bouncing back from difficult circumstances, persistence and consistency are key. Reflect on where you have been and the steps you took to reach your current place. Each decision has shaped your journey. Your prayers will ascend to God's throne, no matter the form or words you use. God hears and responds to the prayers of His children, regardless of how you articulate them.

There are many kinds of prayer, each serving a unique purpose, but all aimed at deepening your relationship with God and advancing His kingdom. Keep in mind that, through persistence in prayer, you are empowered to align your heart with God's will, drawing closer to His divine provision and guidance.

Secret Prayer: In Matthew 6:6, Jesus teaches His disciples about the importance of secret prayer: *"But when you pray, go into your room, close the door and pray to your Father, who is unseen; then your Father, who sees what is done in secret, will reward you openly."*

This verse underscores the profound truth that prayer is not about public displays but about a personal, intimate connection with God. It's not about endless repetition or long, drawn-out sessions. Rather, prayer is about persistently keeping your requests before God, living each day by faith, and trusting that He will answer in His perfect timing.

Living by faith means believing that God will answer your prayers, even if His response is delayed. His delays are never without purpose, they are meant to refine your character, deepen your faith, and increase your hope. The process of persisting in prayer transforms you as much as the answer you seek. It builds endurance, strengthens your relationship with God, and prepares you to receive His blessings.

After you have bounced back from the edge, it's crucial to maintain this consistent practice of prayer. Keep your requests before God, trust in His timing, and remember that every moment spent in prayer contributes to your spiritual growth. Through persistence, you not only move closer to God but also align yourself with His will and purposes.

Your secret prayers, those moments when you seek God alone, will lead to visible rewards—whether through inner peace, spiritual breakthroughs, or answered prayers. Keep engaging in prayer, believing that your Father sees what is done in secret and will reward you openly.

Family Prayer: Family prayer is one of the most powerful practices for nurturing faith within the home. It is not just about individual prayers but about coming together as a family, united in prayer before God. When a family prays together, they invite God's presence into their home, establishing a foundation of spiritual unity and strength. For example, in Acts 10:2, we learn about Cornelius, a devout and God-fearing man, whose family also shared in his faith and commitment to God: *"He gave generously to those in need and prayed to God regularly."* Cornelius not only walked in faith himself but also created an environment where his family was part of his spiritual journey.

Praying in Groups: Matthew 18:20 emphasizes the power and presence of God when believers come together in agreement: *"For where two or three are gathered in my name, there am I with them."* This verse speaks to the profound impact of communal prayer and unity in the body of Christ.

When believers gather together, whether for worship, prayer, or seeking God's guidance in decision-making, they invite God's presence into their midst. This is not only a matter of physical presence but also a spiritual agreement and alignment with God's will. The prayer of two or more is powerful, especially when it is done in the name of Jesus and in alignment with God's Word.

In the context of Matthew 18, *"binding and loosing"* refers to the authority given to the church to make spiritual decisions regarding conflicts among believers. This power is not arbitrary; it is a responsibility that must be exercised with discernment and guided by the Holy Spirit.

- ***Binding*** refers to the act of prohibiting or forbidding something in the spiritual realm. In the context of church discipline or conflict resolution, this could mean taking action to prevent division or sinful behavior from spreading.

- ***Loosing*** refers to the act of permitting or allowing something, particularly in terms of reconciliation and restoration. When the church binds something, it aims to maintain order, peace, and righteousness. When it looses something, it is offering forgiveness, healing, or freedom in Christ.

This process, though potentially challenging, is meant to ensure that God's will is carried out in a way that honors Him and brings about true restoration, whether in relationships between believers or in matters of spiritual discipline. The church should not only have the authority to make these decisions but must also seek God's wisdom through prayer and discernment. This ensures that any action taken is in line with His will, which will have a lasting impact on both the individual and the community.

Public Prayer: In 1 Corinthians 14:14-17, Paul addresses the use of the gift of tongues in public prayer: *"For if I pray in a tongue, my spirit prays, but my mind is unfruitful. So what shall I do? I will pray with my spirit, but I will also pray with my understanding. I will sing with my spirit, but I will also sing with my understanding."* This passage highlights a key principle when it comes to public prayer, particularly in relation to speaking in tongues.

When a person prays in tongues, it is a spiritual communication, but their understanding is not engaged. While the individual is edified in their spirit, the congregation may not be edified unless there is understanding. For this reason, Paul encourages that when a person prays in tongues publicly, they should also pray for the gift of interpretation, so that the congregation can benefit from the prayer.

SUSTENANCE THROUGH FASTING

....

The kind of fast that is truly acceptable to God goes beyond merely abstaining from food. It is accompanied by actions that demonstrate kindness, compassion, and selfless love. For instance, making a sacrifice like keeping an old car another year to increase your offering to the church, giving up an evening to listen to a friend share their burdens, inviting someone over for a meal, choosing to repair an old TV rather than buying a new one, or sending help to a disaster-stricken area are all examples of positive actions. These sacrifices reflect a heart that seeks to assist others in need, as a way to honor God.

God's promises are effective in meeting every condition. The Lord will guide you and lead you out of spiritual drought, but you must seek His guidance when it comes to fasting. Fasting should be in alignment with His divine will. For example, fasting and prayer are powerful ways to humble yourself and honor God. A fast is not just about abstaining from food; it is a day (or days) of affliction for the soul, a time of deep reflection and repentance.

If your fast does not reflect genuine sorrow for sin or lead to true mortification of sin, it is not a true fast. It is essential to inquire what kind of fast pleases God. Simply adopting a somber appearance, bowing down in an outward display of humility, or showing a sad countenance is not the essence of fasting. Instead, the fast should be a reflection of your heart, a sincere effort to align yourself with God's will and to seek His favor through true repentance and love.

You must be just and fair to those who are indebted to you. Don't be overly harsh with them. Instead, loosen the bands of wickedness that bind others. Let go of the burden of unforgiveness, and show mercy to those who owe you money and cannot repay. Break the yoke of slavery and be charitable to those in need.

Another essential aspect of provision is providing food for the hungry. The bread you have earned honestly, whether from your own work or allowances, should be shared. Deny yourself that you might have enough to give to those in need. Additionally, you are called to provide clothing for those who lack it. When you see someone naked, clothe them. Those who have helped others out of trouble will be richly rewarded. These acts of kindness and generosity matter greatly, especially as you seek to make progress in your journey.

Some may pray for daily bread, as in the prayer, *"Give us this day our daily bread."* This bread may not refer to literal, man-made bread; rather, it comes from your Heavenly Father. It is the Word of God, which is sufficient to nourish the souls of men. Unlike earthly bread, it does not go stale or dry. It cannot be bought in stores. It is always fresh and suitable for the hungry soul.

Finally, consider providing lodging for those in need. Take care of the poor, the cast-out and show great acts of kindness by bringing them into your home. Do not forget to entertain strangers. These are the actions you should put into practice, especially on a fast day, when you seek to honor God through self-sacrifice and service to others.

SUSTENANCE IN WORSHIPPING

....

To sustain your spiritual appetite, it is essential to continually give praises to God, especially after emerging from difficult circumstances. Never allow the power of praise to slip from your mind, remembering where God has brought you from and where you could otherwise be. Reflect on the help you received from the Holy Spirit during your time at the edge. It is a privilege to give thanks and to recognize that you could not have made it on your own during those moments of wandering.

Though someone may have given you a word of encouragement during your despair, that word is effective. Every sincere word spoken has the power to change your direction for the right reasons. Your praises are beautiful in the eyes of God. They connect you personally to the Father, transforming wounds, anxiety and disappointment into expressions of gratitude. When you praise God, He pays attention and you will feel His presence in the atmosphere around you.

One morning, as I was praying and praising, it came to my spirit how God had taken me aside to be tested and tried. In the valley, He restored my soul. From that moment on, the atmosphere shifted into a season of worship. He poured into my spirit until I was truly broken and it was there, in that time of prayer, praise, and worship, that I found healing.

These three powerful tools: prayer, praise, and worship are not carnal but mighty through God in pulling down strongholds. They are essential for constant usage, making a profound difference in your spiritual journey. For those who have bounced back from the edge, these tools are invaluable in keeping you on the right path. Praise, for instance, is like the extra fuel that keeps prayer relevant and potent. When your petitions seem to lose their grip, praise bursts through stagnation and leads you into exuberant worship.

God alone deserves to be praised. Offering praise to Him is not a one-time event but a continuous, seasonal practice that keeps the momentum of gratitude flowing. Praise is one of humanity's responses to God's revelation of Himself. The Bible recognizes that men and women, as well as angels and the natural world, are capable of offering praise to God.

However, human praise of God is a central theme in Scripture. True praise is that special form of worship that makes prayer supernatural and meaningful, guiding us to live our lives well. Tomorrow's strength will come, but live in the present. Developing hobbies and a change of activity will keep your spirit fresh. Above all, it is our bound duty to desire to pray and offer praise continually.

'Order my steps in your word O Lord, I have not chosen myself, but you have chosen me O Lord. I will bless you 'O Lord, I will praise your great name, your grace and your

mercies are ever new, ever available through your Son Jesus Christ our deliver and sustainer of life. (John 15:16)

SUSTENANCE THROUGH THANKSGIVING

....

The importance and spiritual benefits of thanksgiving in our prayer life cannot be overstated. The bible tells us God resisted the proud, but gives grace to the humble, (See James 4:6) you may ask how do you become humble? It is done by being thankful, thus a good rule is to be careful or worried for nothing, be prayerful in all things. It is the sin of thankfulness that caused the ancient world to be plunged into the terrible depth of sexual deprave. (See Romans 1:21)

We are to thank God for His work in creation, and for His work of redemption. Giving God thanks is a meaningful and sustaining ingredient in worshipping God. After you have successfully bounced back from the edge, as to say, 'Father thank you for keeping that which I have committed to You, He has not allowed me to go over the edge of my extremities, or under but have brought you back from the edge. Therefore, my gratitude for blessings is my desire, the importance and spiritual benefits produce from thanksgiving in prayers cannot be overemphasized.

Thus, giving thanks is the expression of gratitude to, or appreciation, it should be unceasing, including others in your prayer. May the God of your Lord Jesus Christ the Father of glory, give you the spirit of wisdom and revelation in the knowledge of Him, that the eyes of your understanding may be enlighten, knowing what is the hope of your calling, and the riches of his glory of His inheritance in the saints.

Thanksgiving is described as a spiritual sacrifice of praise offered to God for His goodness and mercies. Also giving thanks is heaven's theme, when all the angels, elders stood before the throne and worshipped God, saying Amen, 'blessed and glory and wisdom, thanksgiving and honor and might, be to our God forever. (See Rev. 7:12)

Whether you may have an expected set back or loss, and your future may seem unknown, trusting Jesus your Savior and Lord, you can be sure of this. He will go with you wherever you go and you should believe it, because God said it! The words from the psalmist *'Deal bountifully with thy servant, that I may live, and keep thy word, open my eyes, that I may behold wondrous things out of thy law.'* (See Psalms 119:17 KJV)

'But you are bound to give thanks always to God for the brethren and beloved of the Lord because God have from the beginning chosen you to salvation through sanctification of the Spirit and belief of the truth.' It is our duty to give thanks! (See 2 Thess. 2:13 KJV)

Thanksgiving should be unceasing for physical changes, and for the healing of spiritual handicaps, the restoration of the desert to fruitfulness, transformations, and encouragement in view of the Lord's return. Thanksgiving should be spontaneous, the apostle declared, *'I thank my God upon every remembrance for the brethren.* (See Phil 1:3 KJV)

Thanksgiving should be given for the ability to discern spiritual things, in every event or circumstances, and for the good He can bring out of the event, even if it is unpleasant. The constant attitude of prayer will help the believer to maintain gratitude in the face of diversity. (See 1Theses 5:18 KJV)

Giving God thanks from a grateful heart is paramount, useful, inspiring and comely, for spiritual health life and all the wonderful benefits. Thanks should be offered from everyone that has breath, even some animals, and trees bowing their heads giving thanks, much less man should give thanks to the Lord for His goodness and mercies endure forever.

PRAYER

....

Dear God my Father, we justified having peace with our self and peace with God, help us Father not to be anxious for nothing, but in everything by prayer and supplication with thanksgiving let our request be made known to God

Father God even the strongest people get tired at times as we are this moment. Thank you for strength in times of challenges. Each generation gets caught in its own problem, but your plans embraces all generations. Lord you are the only one who sees personally, into the lives, a hundred years from now as clearly as years go'. Lord we thank you!!

Chapter

SHARING YOUR STORY

Everyone has a story to tell and more often than not, is looking for an attentive listener, someone who is inclined to listen without interruption. Finding that person can seem difficult, as many people are more interested in their own stories. Nevertheless, it's important to appreciate and give thanks for the opportunity to share your story, reflecting on how far you've come. The freedom to share your experiences is possible because of what you've been through, even when you had no idea what would become of you while struggling at the edge of disgrace, shame and low self-esteem.

Most people are blessed with the ability to speak, yet many choose not to tell their story. This may stem from past disappointments, perhaps from not being believed or accepted because of who you are or where you've been. It's essential to share your story without imposing your situation on others, with no expectation that they will listen without questions. People may ask about the cause of your dilemma, where it happened, how long it lasted and what steps you took to overcome it.

Nonetheless, your story is yours to share and it holds the power to inspire, heal and create connections with others who may have walked similar paths.

When attempting to win the lost for Christ, be mindful not to send mixed messages that could cause fear or confusion. Making personal changes for the better can be difficult, and if not approached with care, it might deter someone from making the right decision. All people need to rely on the help of the Holy Spirit to convict their hearts and guide them in making the decision to accept God's plan for salvation.

A young man once shared his story of how he was ridiculed by people he trusted for many years, which led him to a point of hopelessness; he was ready to give up for good. He had lost faith in both God and people. However, at the right moment, he reached out and cried out for help. It was then that he found renewed hope and a desire to share this hope with others. He began telling others about the hope of his calling, about how Jesus died for humanity to reconcile them to God the Father.

He shared this story of love and empathy with everyone he encountered in his daily life and you should do the same. Everyone is interested in love stories, but this one is exceptional and unlike any other. He recognized the need to develop a plan that could reach others, starting with those closest to him. He shared his story with one person at a time, then two and gradually, his message reached more and more people. His hope was that each person who heard the story would go on to share it with others. Over time, the storyteller's influence grew, eventually becoming a community center of hope.

'What was the story about?'

The story centers around the birth, death, and resurrection of Jesus. These were the main subjects. He told the story in simple, layman's terms, gradually progressing to a deeper understanding. He explained how Jesus was born on earth through a simple virgin. Jesus' earthly mother was named Mary and His earthly father was Joseph. After an exhausting journey on a donkey, Joseph and his pregnant wife Mary did not check into the master suite of a grand hotel. Instead, they had to settle for a humble animal shelter, as there was no place for them in the inn. Mary gave birth without the aid of modern painkillers or sterilized environments.

Yet, the bravest woman remained silent while giving birth. Jesus grew up as a normal child until the early years of accountability. God, your heavenly Father, had a designated plan for everyone on the planet to fulfill, a plan that would be carried out as they grew. Though Mary, Jesus' earthly parent, knew nothing about this divine plan, what difference would it have made if she had known?

God set His eternal plan in motion by sending Jesus to earth as the Redeemer of lost people. The plan was for Jesus to give His life to redeem humanity and restore fellowship with His Father, since humanity had broken that fellowship through disobedience. The act of dying by crucifixion was part of this plan; Jesus would would be nailed to a cross and killed, all for the sake of His Father's love for humanity.

A love as strong as death. There is no greater love than this: that someone lays down his life for his friends. Jesus' dead body was taken down from the cross, where He had been nailed, and buried in a newly borrowed tomb. After three days, the same Jesus rose from the grave on the third day and appeared to many who were expecting Him to

Sharing Your Story

rise from the dead, though many doubted His story, even today. But it matters not.

In times when you feel anxious and afraid, searching for a faithful friend to share your story can be a challenge. When anxiety grabs hold of your mind like a powerful force, "phone a friend," take action, and gather the courage to face your fears. Recall former sermons you have heard about God and His promises, that He will take care of you. This reminder will be sufficient to ease the anxiety and keep you from slipping back to the edge. Never fear falling or being unsure of where you may land or how hard the fall might be. Rest assured, God will come to your rescue and spread His everlasting wings beneath you. Falling into God's arms is nothing to fear.

The way forward to becoming an overcomer of negative fear is to confront it. Maintain regular private and open conversations with your faithful friend. Be open and share your feelings with them consistently. Likewise, go tell your story, go listen, and become a good listener. Just as you hope someone will listen to you, you should also be willing to listen to their story.

Life is a process of giving and taking. While some individuals expect to receive, they may not be prepared to give in return. Certainly, it is understood that you cannot give what you do not have. For example, sharing the Good News can be a difficult subject for many, depending on their lifestyle or culture.

From the very beginning, you may sense whether your message will fall on deaf ears or be unwelcome. However, do not be overly concerned about this. Your primary duty is to tell and share the Good News with as many as possible. It is not ordinary news, like the daily reports about what's happening in the world; no, it is the Good News of salvation. It is about how the world was in darkness, but Jesus, the Son of God, came and turned on the light so that all could see.

He did not just turn on the light and leave men in darkness; He said, *"Let there be light"* and invited people to come to the light, to see themselves and eventually see Him. He calls for their attention, though men often love darkness rather than light. There is a vast need for mankind to hear and share the Good News, especially after bouncing back from the edge. This message is truly mind-blowing.

To make this message even more impactful, consider seeking others with similar desires and interests: messengers who can help spread the Good News and draw attention from others. Perhaps you could post a sign in a designated area to highlight your message: *"Urgently seeking tellers. Apply within."* There is great benefit in sharing your story. How secure and confident are you in telling it?

When someone else has a great idea, you should support them and celebrate their success. To be an effective storyteller, you must make your listeners feel secure and valued. This involves expressing genuine love and affection for others and taking delight in honoring them.

For example, Jesus spoke words that transformed lives. He understood that preoccupied minds don't always listen attentively. Many people preferred to hear His stories rather than respond to His requests. Yet, if you are someone accustomed to listening only to the facts and not the person expressing them, it's time to change your focus and truly listen.

The call to *"go tell"* everyone you meet about the extraordinary news of the Kingdom of Heaven remains vital. "The Kingdom of Heaven is at hand." Share how those who desire to inherit the kingdom must be born again, receiving legal rights as citizens of the kingdom and practicing its laws. Proclaim the truth of the Kingdom, where Christ is Sovereign. This is a Kingdom of Heaven, not of this world.

The man telling this remarkable story may have seemed ordinary, with nothing special about him to be desired or listened to. He was like one crying out in the wilderness, all alone with no friends to talk to, but with a great conviction from the One who sent him. He was not eloquently dressed or well-presented in his attire. His surroundings were inhospitable, yet he proclaimed that he was sent by God to prepare the way for someone more important than he was.

The people who heard him were extremely proud of their privileges and insensible to their sin. They belittled the man telling his story, but he was sent to take down their high opinion of themselves. His message was one of repentance and humility, pointing them toward the right way. It was believed that the Kingdom of God would soon appear in its own time. There were many who eagerly listened, but only a few true believers. Nevertheless, the story had to be told, whether the people heard or whether they rejected it.

When reflecting on the consequences of not sharing the Good News, consider this: How will people change their understanding of what is right if they never hear

Sharing Your Story

the message? It is vitally important to tell your story to as many people as you can. Share how something miraculous happened, something that could have cost you your life or your privileges, when you were on the brink of despair, hopelessness and fatigue. Thankfully, your life was spared during those dark moments, giving you the chance to come back from the edge.

Use this opportunity to go tell, go pray, and fast for the benefit of others, offering a warning: *"Take heed, turn from your sinful ways, and reform your lives."*

There are inscribable and special benefits in keeping your spiritual skills sharpened by the experiences you've encountered while waiting by the edge. Consider that when you were brought back from the edge, it wasn't due to your own merit; it was for God's specific purposes for your life. Good skills are granted to those who know who they are and what they are about. Skills such as caring and sharing are not intended for heartless, selfish individuals who are only interested in themselves. Such people would not care if others live or die.

God gave you His wonderful gifts without measure, skills that can be multiplied by sharing with others. Don't believe that these gifts will run dry, for He gives and will keep on giving as long as you keep sharing. This may not be fully understood until you give what has been given to you freely.

LIVING VICTORIOUSLY

....

The term *"victory"* originally applies to warfare and denotes the success achieved in personal combat or through military operations. When success is achieved in a military campaign, it constitutes a strategic victory, while success in smaller engagements is considered a tactical victory. In the context of nations at war, each side is fighting to secure victory and often, one side wins while the other loses. Victory therefore, is a winning outcome and it's a moment of celebration when one team triumphs over another, with spectators cheering joyously as they jump for joy.

Living victoriously means living in a state of continuous triumph; getting over setbacks, bouncing back from stagnation, and ultimately living a victorious life after overcoming challenges. It involves consistency, keen reflection, focus, character-building, and maintaining progress, even in seemingly impossible situations. There are no shortcuts, no automatic solutions and certainly no quick fixes. Achieving victory requires a close relationship with the Holy Spirit, who helps you maintain patience, steadiness, long-suffering and a renewed mindset.

The importance of building a right and healthy relationship with God through His Son, Jesus, is both vital and necessary for daily living. This relationship must become a habit and a lifestyle, not just a short-term effort, but a consistent way of life. You need a sensitive and active conscience that speaks to your spirit, especially when you begin to stray.

Neglecting prayer, meditation, Bible reading, and consideration for others can hinder your spiritual growth. Instead, strive to change your attitude, improve your actions, and grow in watchfulness and alertness. Look to Jesus, the author and perfecter of your faith, for guidance and strength.

In doing so, you will develop a personal history of victories over impossibilities and hindrances. You'll be able to reflect on the many challenges that could have led to disaster, but instead, you successfully bounced back from the edge. It becomes an exciting time of drawing from past experiences, where each victory serves as a reminder of

God's grace and faithfulness. Living to tell your story and share these blessings is a gift, and through it, you maintain your reasons not to quit. Instead, you live victoriously, praising and giving thanks to God, the giver of life.

Remember that true victory comes from maintaining a positive attitude toward your opponents, wishing them well in their endeavors. Reflect on the story of a young boy who faced a giant, far larger than any normal man. The boy seemed an unlikely match for this towering opponent, yet he held victory in his mind. He was determined to win.

The giant boasted loudly, proclaiming all he would do to the boy, but the lad remained silent, relying solely on the help of his God. With remarkable simplicity and faith, the boy won the victory, slaying the giant with just one small stone he had picked from the brook. *Wow!* What a powerful reminder of how, with God's help, even the most overwhelming challenges can be overcome!

Victory is not granted to those with a lazy or careless disposition, nor to boastful individuals. Certainly not. Winning the victory is not for the faint-hearted. It comes through battling for something tangible and meaningful, where effort and dedication have been demonstrated.

Some people prepare themselves for battle, fighting wholeheartedly. Those who achieve victory are not cowards but bold warriors striving for a worthy cause. They are willing to give their lives to be counted among the victors. Some may never return to tell their story, but they are nonetheless remembered as winners.

Victory is so impressive that these warriors would rather leave those they love behind to strive intentionally for it, than to be counted among the losers. While others stood on the edge of despair, rejected, disappointed, with empty pockets and nowhere to call home. They fought their inner demons rather than step toward the edge. No, they fought to obtain victory.

It's a sweet story to read of victory, especially for those who may have never been inclined to listen. These are the people who, despite the odds, have explored their full potential and are now ready for the next level. They don't merely boast about their victory, but hold it in their hearts as they seek the next adventure toward triumph.

You must never become overly impressed with what you've already accomplished; there is still so much more within you. When God brought you back from the edge, it was to make a difference. You did not come back empty.

You came filled with potential, discovering the freedom to do exploits for God.

Never stop or park your dreams, allowing your potential to remain idle. Go tell, go share. There are inquisitive listeners all around, eager to hear how you made it back from the edge and became victorious. You, yes, you, listen to the drumbeat of your heart, follow its rhythm, and take one step at a time toward your victory.

Having victory over circumstances is fully functional, having five principles of the overcoming obstacles. For example, dreams that are never to come to pass, ideas that have never been shared should have never been put on hold for longer than they should. A splendid and important gift from God, you are God's gift to the world. Your hands are given to write what is downloaded in your spirit and asks God for the passion to reach the unreachable and minister to their needs. That's victory! Develop that idea until it becomes a reality ready to launch into victory.

Establishing a firm foundation begins by building an atmosphere of growth within your heart and mind. Strive to get the right mix, aiming at your goals with intentionality. When you approach something, do so with full commitment and determination to reach victory.

Conversing with others who have attained victory and hearing their experiences can be adaptable and insightful. Try to see things from their point of view, rather than starting a conversation by focusing on yourself.

When seeking connections, find common ground with others through their background, experiences, and adapt your approach to fit them, rather than expecting them to adapt to you. Instead of immediately telling people how you feel, take the time to understand how they feel. By capturing the experiences of others, you can show them how they too, can achieve victory and encourage them to maintain discipline in their own quest.

Victory requires consistency. You cannot keep stopping and starting. You must remain steadfast, driven by a strong desire to succeed. Cultivate a willingness to learn new skills every day and apply what you have already learned.

Victorious living is pure, without hidden agendas, flaws, or questionable motives. While the past may be filled with both good and bad memories, it's essential to avoid carrying negative reflections into the present. Life's victory isn't built solely on good moments, but rather on a mindset that focuses on the positives. Be selective and make the right choices, deciding what ideas should stay and which should go.

There can never be victory without challenges, whether they are obstacles in war, misunderstandings, negative thoughts, or difficult behavior. Much like good athletes striving to reach the finish line, these challenges can serve as stepping stones toward victory. They are tests designed to reveal the strength and determination of those who are striving for success.

If you come across someone fervently chasing their ambition, offer them a word of caution: encourage them to earnestly seek patience, tenacity, and wisdom from above, for these qualities are far more effective than sheer willpower alone. Without them, frustration will inevitably await, ready to mock and say, *"I told you so."*

To silence the doubters and prove them wrong, you must draw from every reserve of positivity. Plant your feet firmly, stand strong and declare with unwavering confidence: *"I've put your name… there."*

PRAYER

....

Dear God, I ask for courage to face the future, and wisdom to live victoriously when the tide changes. "I can do all things through Christ who strengthens me."

Father, I'm tired of going through life with no real purpose, as it brings no glory to You. You have created everything, including me, to bring You pleasure. I know You have a specific purpose for me. Your Word says, "You have formed me in the womb to be Your servant."

Father God, at the end of my life, I want to look back and say to Jesus, "I brought glory to You here on earth." Although I've brought grief to my earthly father, I am doing my best to rectify everything and walk honestly before You.

Father God, today I push aside my worries and take a moment to give thanks with a grateful heart for every blessing I've received, for the provision that always arrives at the hour I need it. Thank You for the love that embraces the worst in me, for Your humbling mercy and for Your unstoppable grace. You have blessed me far beyond what I deserve.

In Jesus' precious name, I pray. Amen!

Chapter 16

CELEBRATING A COME BACK

Times of celebration may only emerge during special seasons and occasions, yet there are moments that are uniquely marked just for you. Everyone has their own reasons for celebrating, whether it's achievements like passing exams, the birth of a new child, accomplishments of family and friends, new jobs, properties, locations, cars, or something else. Let's celebrate by doing something special or enjoyable, such as occasionally going on holiday or going out for dinner.

Celebrating a *'comeback'* from the edge is one of the most glorious events an individual can ever experience. It's like a person rising from the dead to live again. Some can testify how they once felt dead inside, living lives of unfulfillment with no satisfaction. It could have felt like being on a stormy sea or living without hope for tomorrow, uncertain of what would happen in the next hour or day.

Like a blind date, uncertain if it will come to fruition, or living in fear and doubt, the only hope is to hope in something called Hopefulness with a capital H and all the letters that follow. Now, it's a new day, a time to celebrate life, an abundant and victorious life. When people are purged of wrongdoings, there is great relief and hope. No matter how difficult your experience was, you can look forward to the day of celebration when God will completely restore you. It will surely be a day of cheer, bouncing back from the edge.

Celebrating a joyful and happy time of laughter and sometimes feasting, as when a father's son returns home safe and sound, with no scratches on his body and no limbs lost, apart from the instability in his mind caused by worrying about what the people in the community might say. His father was not perturbed by what others had to say or criticize about his wayward son returning home safely. He ignored them all, knowing that it was the right decision for his son to return home.

He then ordered the servants to prepare and kill the fatted calf, as he arranged for music and dancing to celebrate the safe return of his son. It was a mixture of joy, happiness, and community spirit that swept from the young to the old. Everyone was infused with the spirit of celebration as they welcomed the youth home from the edge of destruction to a safe environment. They couldn't remember the last time they had seen Raymond, until that bright and sunny day when they heard music coming from the house. Surprised, they took the liberty of joining in the celebration. *"Home at last!"*

The song selected was:

"Amazing grace, how sweet the sound, that saved a wretch like Raymond, I once was lost, but now I'm found, Was blind, but now I see."

Lord, thank you for the gift of this day. I will celebrate Your goodness and enjoy each moment of it. Lord, regardless of what comes my way today, You will defend, protect and vindicate me. So, this day, I will walk in Your joy, favor, mercy, guidance, protection and blessing.

The reason for celebrating should resonate continuously in one's mind as a meaningful event. The reaction of struggling out of something or somewhere is remarkably significant. Its as if to say, "Remember the experience. Don't you dare forget!"

CELEBRATING BOUNCING FROM THE EDGE

....

Bouncing back from the edge can definitely be a joyful time of realisation, recognising what could have happened had it not been for one's destiny to live and embrace life. It is about putting up a fight for survival, refusing to let go and holding on. Only Raymond's father knew how much it cost in sleepless nights, praying and hoping that his son was still alive and hadn't been devoured by ravenous beasts or killed by evil men. He understood the importance of time, watching intently through every crack in the door and window, hoping his son would remember to come home. Sometimes, it was torturous, waiting for the morning of another day.

A massive and unforgettable event, like bouncing back from broken pieces, is something that can never truly be described or explained in just a few words to someone who has never been in such a situation. They simply wouldn't understand the logic behind the desire to get it right, especially when every attempt seems to make things worse. You can imagine the frustration, particularly when you're alone in a limited space.

A celebration of returning from the edge of danger, despair, loneliness, false hope, regrets, rebellion, sickness, mental illness and failures, is a special time for those involved. Each person experiences their own unique story, facing different challenges at the edge. Some light-hearted individuals may have made themselves comfortable sitting near the edge, refusing to do anything for themselves, until one precious day when their mindset shifts and they finally start helping themselves.

CHRISTMAS CELEBRATION

The world's happiness is often evoked by the unwrapping of gifts on Christmas morning, strolling hand in hand with a loved one, or being surprised on your birthday. It can come from laughing at a comedian's joke or taking a holiday to an exotic location. Everyone seeks happiness and many make it a lifelong pursuit by spending money, collecting things and searching for new experiences. But if happiness depends solely on circumstances, what happens when the toys rust, loved ones pass away, health deteriorates, money is stolen and the party ends? What is left? Happiness fades and disappears.

The real meaning of the Christmas celebration is much deeper. Some believe it is on the 25th of December that we mark the birth of Christ, the true reason for the season. It's a time when families gather in churches, homes, pubs and community centers to celebrate the Christmas events. For anyone observing, they might wonder what all the hustle and bustle is about.

Yet sadly, for some, Christmas is just another day of the year. It's a time when they don't have enough food to feed themselves and their families. As they watch others fill their shopping carts with treats for their celebrations, they might wish for the same abundance, unaware that not everyone is fortunate enough to experience that joy.

NEW YEAR CELEBRATIONS

....

New Year's Day, falling on the 1st of January, symbolizes new beginnings and the opportunity to start over again. For many, it's a time to turn over a new page, leaving behind the struggles and mistakes of the past year. There's no magic in the turning of the calendar, but there is power in choosing to move forward, learning from last year's missteps, failures, and experiences. The start of a new year often brings resolutions, promises to live differently or strive for self-improvement in the days, months and years ahead.

While making resolutions can be meaningful, it can also be wise to take one day at a time. The key is not to overwhelm yourself with unrealistic expectations but to live each day with intention, embracing the potential for growth, learning and positive change. Living with great expectation for a better future gives purpose to each new day, no matter the challenges that arise.

CELEBRATING A WEDDING ANIVERSARY

....

Celebrating a wedding anniversary is an extraordinary bash for both the young and older married partners. It is a special time of celebrating, exchanging gifts and renewal of vows. This meaningful event is precious to the couple as it marks how far they came through and are yet still devoted to each other, as the vow to hold it together for another year. I listened attentively to an individual giving, as it were, a marriage lecture to friends that were interested in the subject. Apparently she said her marriage was was a faultless marriage! Bless her, but not realizing that her listeners may not be so fortunate, they might have some disagreement valleys to cross, some conversations to be had, and possible the most important thing, to plan saying 'sorry' to each other for being so rude the other day.

I thought it was interesting at her particular point of positivity in her marriage and praying with others for a few years she can still be singing off the same song sheet. As a marriage matures, there should be more love and freedom between partners, as the wife takes the imitative for love-making. Many cultures have role stereotypes of the roles men and women play in love-making but the security of true love with both married partners is the freedom to imitate acts of love and express their true feelings.

CELEBRATING A NEW BIRTH

After a woman carries an unborn child for nine months inside the womb, there comes a time to give birth. Afterwards, it is a time of celebration. An additional human, whether it's a boy or a girl, is a blessing. For the family, it is an exciting event: children's and adults' birthdays. This kind of celebration can become extremely expensive, leaving no money to cover other household bills, but as long as people have a good time, nothing else matters.

BORN AGAIN CELEBRATION

It is not often spoken about today, yet this is one of the most important celebrations: being converted and born again as a new person. It is like waking up from darkness into light, where the stars are bright and dreams that were once overlaid by disappointments suddenly spring up like a new day. You are born into the family of God. Many people from all walks of life may have already experienced the new birth, just like a newborn infant coming into a family. Friends will want to join in the celebration to see this new convert. The new birth, otherwise called regeneration, is a process of growth, knowledge, change, fruitfulness, victory and often, discipline. As newborn babies desire the pure milk of the word, that you may grow thereby. As born-again believers, we are to seek to mature in the midst of hardship and grow in discipline, obedience and relentless focus on our purpose.

CELERBATING WATER BAPTISM

....

The newly born-again believer, after conversion, decides to be baptised in water, fulfilling the step of receiving Jesus Christ as Lord of their life. They are immersed in water in the name of the Father, Son, and Holy Spirit. Families and friends joyfully come to witness this celebration and rejoice in the freedom of the newly baptised convert entering God's family. This event symbolises burying the old deeds and rising up out of the water with new minds and a new intention to live in the fullness of life found only in Jesus Christ. The traditional baptismal service involves full immersion in a pool of water, with the baptiser and assistant playing their roles. Some organisations conduct baptismal services by sprinkling water over the candidate's head, rather than immersing them.

CELEBRATING VALENTINES DAY

The month of February marks a time for lovers, where people remember falling in love, engagements, marriages, celebrating love and happiness, exchanging beautiful gifts with one another. The Valentine season is when love steps up to a higher level, allowing partners to shine and bloom again, even in the darkest evening shadows. It's a time for renewing marriage vows, stirring up current relationships and adding a little more spark to make the love shine brighter. It's a time to pay special attention to body language and get closer. Renewed promises and conversations are seen as more serious and meaningful.

CELEBRATING EASTER

....

Easter varies each year; sometimes it falls in March, other times in April. Regardless of the date, Easter commemorates the day when God sent Jesus to the cross to cancel your past. He nailed every record of the charges against you to the cross, removed every trace of offense from your record, and declared it fully paid. Easter is an annual celebration of this great event, but it should not become just another ritual that does little to satisfy the needs of the heart.

The resurrection of Christ must become the center of this historical act of reflection. It must become a personal reality to each believer. This is called love, unmerited favor, a love demonstrated without asking for anything in return from the one who gave it.

Christians celebrate the Easter season to honor Jesus' return from the grave, never to die again. He came back triumphantly, breaking all protocols of earth and hell. All human plans were knocked out for good, yet the Savior of humanity came back, carrying the evidence of victory over the edge. Everyone who believes in Him is redeemed by the blood of the cross.

CELEBRATING MOTHER'S DAY

The Bible refers to every aspect of motherhood. The virtues of motherhood are often extolled, including the compassion for children and the sorrow that comes with them. The fact that God would use a human mother to bring His Son into the world has bestowed upon motherhood its greatest honor.

Mother's Day is a special event celebrated in most churches and some organisations take the time to honor mothers. Children, grandchildren, great-grandparents, stepchildren and foster children all come together to celebrate their mothers. It's a time when children show love and appreciation for their mothers. They reflect on their upbringing, how their mothers cared for and loved them without hesitation and acknowledge that they will never be able to repay their mothers for their devotion.

CELEBRATING FATHER'S DAY

Who is a father? A father is a male parent, the head of the household. Fathers are providers for the welfare of their offspring and in return, children celebrate Father's day in style and appreciation. A father is expected to love, give instruction and provide discipline in the home and in schools. Some communities, through school boards, share ideas on how to help groom youngsters in the right direction.

Most children, whether young or old, celebrate Father's day in style, in churches or through various organizations. Fathers are well known for showing leadership, serving as role models and exemplifying high moral standards, both in words and deeds.

CELEBRATING VETERAN'S DAY

The celebration of war heroes who made it back from fighting for their country is a grand occasion. These soldiers willingly went and fought battles for their countries.

At the end of the conflict, some return safely, while others may have succumbed to injuries or death. However, credit should also be given to their families for their efforts in sacrificing their time and lives for a worthy cause.

CELEBRATING BLACK HISTORY MONTH

People from around the world celebrate Black History Month in October each year, marking the history of immigrants invited to the United Kingdom to assist in building the country's economy. This period is often referred to as the "Windrush" era. Some families gathered in one place to enjoy the opportunities of a new country and adopted new cultures in a strange land, while others chose to return rather than adapt. Some have never lived long enough to tell their own stories of what they experienced during those years of Windrush and how they overcame the challenges.

Black History Month has become an appealing event each year, with the celebration extending to other nationalities who are now embracing the meaning of the Windrush experience. People gather in various parts of the world to celebrate and share memories. Though many of the people who lived through the trauma of Windrush have passed away due to sickness or old age, the celebration continues every year.

PRAYER

Father in heaven, I lift up Your great name; You are worthy to be praised from the rising of the sun to its going down. I thank You for taking us through the various challenges of life, especially for giving us the opportunity to bounce back from the edge of all sorts of difficult experiences and bringing us to higher levels of independence, where we can recognize Your faithfulness. May Your Holy Spirit locate us in our hour of loss and despair, guiding us with Your comforting presence and strength.

In Jesus' name, Amen.

Chapter 17

RE-ADJUSTING AFTER THE EDGE

If you have been accustomed to walking obediently in God's will but have experienced a setback or fallen away, now is the time to regain your spiritual footing and return to a life aligned with His purpose. Acknowledge the need to reconnect and rebuild your relationship with God. Unless you dedicate time to reading His Word, you will struggle to maintain a lifestyle that pleases Him. This process requires obedience and discipline to reframe your mindset, letting go of old habits and embracing a life filled with God's peace and joy.

You may have made countless mistakes and caused harm to yourself or others. These missteps likely did not happen overnight or by accident, though they may not have been intentional either. Despite it all, your experiences have not placed you beyond the reach of God's grace. His mercy has no expiration date and He remains faithful and able to do far more than you can ask, imagine, or hope for. Let this truth be your anchor as you choose to return to Him.

If someone falls badly, it's often described as having *"crashed and burned."* When something burns, all that remains is ashes. Similarly, when you fail (and at some point, everyone does), turning to God allows Him to restore you. He can use your failures as opportunities to strengthen you and propel you forward. Your life may feel useless or devoid of hope today, but if you turn to God and make the necessary adjustments, He can create something beautiful out of your mess.

The secret to victory lies in letting God transform your mistakes into testimonies for His glory and lessons for your future. Rather than dwelling on regrets, cultivate a positive attitude and work towards a meaningful and constructive life. Every person has a responsibility to contribute, no matter how small or seemingly insignificant their efforts may appear. Success may not come immediately, but persistence and determination are essential. Keep trying, and give your best effort.

The Bible doesn't just promise long life; it also promises a life of quality, peace, and prosperity when you keep God's commandments in your heart. While others may view life negatively, each person has the capacity to change their mindset and embrace wisdom, which will add meaning and length to their days. It's easy to get caught up in life's distractions, adopting bad habits, and overlooking what is right. However, refocusing on what truly matters, seeking first the things of God, can lead to transformation.

To experience this change, you must be born again into God's family, becoming part of a team committed to living in alignment with His will. Let this be your step towards renewal and purpose.

Now that you have overcome the pain and returned from an abnormal lifestyle, it's time to focus on developing and forming new habits. Start by getting a pad and pen to jot down a simple plan for managing your daily time. This plan should guide you without becoming a burden: if you don't manage your time effectively, it can take control of you, like an unreasonable schoolmaster.

You don't need to dedicate your entire morning to this. Choose a time that works best for you, whether it's in the morning, at noon, or in the evening. Spend just a few minutes creating a routine and committing to making it a daily habit.

Instead of rigidly adhering to a specific time allocation, consider setting aside just half an hour each day for reading, praying and meditating on the Bible in small portions. Take the time to jot down key verses and reflect on their meaning. Ponder what each verse is saying to you personally and remember to invite the Holy Spirit to guide you, providing insight and understanding into what He wants to reveal to you.

As someone who has escaped the edge and bounced back to a sense of normality, you are encouraged to meditate on Scripture and engage in prayer with sincerity and faith. Confess your failures openly and truthfully to your Heavenly Father, seeking His forgiveness with a heart full of trust in His promise to hear your prayers. Remember to include others in your prayers, such as family, friends, well-wishers, those who are sick and even government leaders. This practice can be approached in different sessions, allowing you to focus on various aspects of your spiritual journey and intercessions.

Adjusting your mindset to fit your circumstances can lead to great progress. For instance, getting up a little

Re-Adjusting After The Edge

earlier each morning to focus on your intentions might work wonders for you. This small adjustment can help you achieve your goals and create a sense of accomplishment.

As you experience growth, others may notice and inquire about the secret of your success. You will find joy in sharing how an organized and intentional day can lead to meaningful achievements and positively impact one's life.

Although succeeding does not necessarily mean you are in the will of God, and others may think you are right, your plans and goals should instead emerge from the vision God has given you. There is only one appropriate response to God's plan: obedience. Partial or delayed obedience is, in essence, disobedience.

One of the most difficult lessons to learn is that God is sovereign; He is above all those who hold authority. He sets limits on the power of governments, businesses and religious leaders worldwide. Those who live in freedom and enjoy a relatively high degree of independence often find this truth challenging to comprehend.

When you set your own goals, you may lack heartfelt confidence that God is doing the work, and you might feel that it's all up to you. However, when you trust God to bring things to pass, you can confidently readjust to normality. Having good intentions for how to re-adjust your life requires listening to the voice of God more attentively, maintaining clear, positive thinking and learning how to confront each of your fears by using and believing in the word of God. Look for the facts about what you fear to remove the misinformation, and instead of focusing on the phobia, focus on the promises of God: *"I will never leave you, I will strengthen you, and I will uphold you with my righteous right hand."*

As your faith in God grows, you will experience tremendous weakening of your fears. They will become weaker. A peacefulness and freedom from fear, which will surpass all human understanding, will come upon you. Re-adjust your long-term vision and cultivate openness and confidence. Have a conversation with yourself. Become a good listener. Keep your vision close to your heart, being selective about with whom you share it. Create an inner circle of trusted friends, ideally those with the same intentions.

For instance, when a person has a vision, you should be eager to understand what to do with it. Reflect on the potential you were born to fulfill in all areas of your vision. Now that you have bounced back from setbacks, start by focusing on the most important tasks, then gradually expand and master them. Having a clear vision of what you would like to become at a specific time or in a particular endeavor, work towards it and ask yourself,

"What kind of history would I like to be remembered for through my dreams?

How much time am I willing to invest in my vision?

What kind of history am I making?"

Your vision needs to be something that cannot be easily erased, creating lasting value.

For example, Nelson Mandela's vision took him into prison, where he spent years in solitary confinement. Nevertheless, he emerged with his vision intact and even became bolder than he was when first imprisoned. He made up his mind to die trying to fulfill his purpose.

RIGHT DECISIONS

....

The previous chapters spoke of a son's attitude who made the wrong decision concerning his father. The name of that son was Raymond. He said to his father, *"Give me the share of my inheritance,"* so that he could go and have fun in the wide world. This son was not a street boy and had no experience living outside his father's house. It must have grieved and greatly concerned his caring father, knowing the potential consequences for his son. Raymond received what he asked for and went out quickly. He spent it all without any thought of investing or saving for a rainy day.

Immediately, the son felt a surge of selfishness, power, and pride, believing he had become the master of his own destiny. But it is a fact that pride goes before destruction, and a haughty spirit leads to a fall. Raymond did not ask his father for any advice on what to do with the money he received, nor did he inquire about how he should spend it.

As a wise father, although he did not want his young son to leave home, he could have given the best advice and fatherly instructions. But Raymond didn't ask. Perhaps he thought he knew it all and would never fall into want. He was not too young to learn the importance of wisdom, yet, though he was crushed and perplexed on every side, his only hope was, *"My father is praying for me!"*

COMPARATIVE OF INTEREST

Jason was the son of a wealthy father who owned vast properties, land and endless cattle. His father left him an abundance of flocks and herds. Jason was an obedient lad, his ways were delightful and pleasing to his father, as well as to his heavenly Father, who saw what was in his heart. Jason knew that one day he would become an excellent king, ruling over His people and so he was in preparation for his future role.

One night, as Jason was sound asleep, he had a dream. In the dream, he was asked to request whatever he wanted, whatever was in his heart or desire. He wondered why the question came at night and may never have understood the reason. However, Jason responded earnestly, *"Give me wisdom, knowledge, and understanding."* The request may have seemed simple, yet it was of a different nature.

What would be the benefit of asking for temporal blessings without the wisdom to manage them? Thankfully, Jason asked for spiritual blessings, which are purposeful and lasting. Though Jason was very ambitious and loved God, acknowledging His great goodness toward his father, there existed a close-knit father and son relationship. Jason sought to follow his father's example closely.

God had asked him to request anything he wanted, in humble recognition of his deficiency. Jason pleaded, "Lord, I am but a little child. I do not know how to go out or come in as I should; nor can I do the daily work to assist my father." Men's character often shows in their choices and desires. Like a genuine son, Jason chose spiritual blessings over temporal ones. His petition was, *"Give me the faculty of understanding,"* in other words, *"Give me my father's spirit; let Your promise to my father be established in me."*

Jason begged God to give him an understanding heart: *"Give therefore Thy servant an understanding heart."* The answer God gave to his request was a pleasing one. God saw that Jason preferred spiritual blessings rather than temporal ones. But that was not all, it was a prevailing prayer, and it prevailed for more than he had asked. God gave him wisdom, insight, foresight and added riches and honor

Re-Adjusting After The Edge

beyond what he could have imagined. These are God's gifts to all who seek first His kingdom (Matt. 6:33).

The value of wisdom brings happiness and happy is the man who finds it. It is important not to forget to seek wisdom or to turn away from the words of God. Wisdom is the principal thing and in all your getting, add understanding. Men and women cannot attain ethical wisdom on their own; they must first acknowledge the Lord in all their ways, and He will direct their paths. Wisdom should be acquired because it produces good fruits and ensures stability.

Biblical wisdom is practical, not theoretical and many will benefit from it. It will keep you from evil. It is far better than rubies and it is more valuable than gold. It is good to prefer grace over gold in all things because godliness has the promise of both this life and the life to come. However, the life that is now does not promise godliness, but wisdom and grace will bring either outward prosperity or sweeten the absence of it.

God promised Jason riches and honor, but only if he walked in His ways as his father did. Unfortunately, Jason failed to meet the conditions and did not receive the promised length of days, even though he had riches to enjoy. The way to obtain spiritual blessings is to be persistent in prayer, wrestling with God for them as Jason did. He asked for that one most important thing and the rest followed.

To obtain temporal blessings, one must be indifferent to them and put God first, preferring Him over all else. Jason received wisdom because he did not ask for riches and wealth, realising that wisdom is better than gold. The riches of this world are temporal and will soon pass away, but the wisdom that comes from God abides forever and lasts through generations. Trusting God, and leaning not on your own understanding, will lead to the fulfillment of your desires when you acknowledge God in all your ways.

GODLY WISDOM

....

Godly wisdom is an excellent gift, and you are encouraged to seek the wisdom necessary for godly living. When Jason received wisdom from God, it was favorable for his ministry. His first test was how to effectively use the wisdom God had given him. He was presented with a very difficult case that required divine wisdom to resolve. Two women, both harlots, came to him seeking justice for a troubling situation. The women, who lived together, had both given

Re-Adjusting After The Edge

birth to sons within three days of each other. During the night, one of the women accidentally smothered her child and upon realizing the child was dead, she secretly exchanged the dead baby with the other woman's living child.

Although she knew the truth, she sought public justice, claiming the living child as her own, while accusing the other woman of having the dead child. The case was difficult to resolve and the key question was: who was the true mother of the living child? The two women were vehement in their claims, each showing deep concern for the living child. Neither woman would claim the dead child, although it would be easier to bury it than to care for the living one. The neighbors, who had been present at the births and had even performed circumcisions, could not recall any distinguishing features between the two children.

Jason patiently listened to both women. After hearing their arguments, the spirit of wisdom revealed the truth to him. He called for a sword and ordered that the living child be divided between the two women. This would test the reactions of both women and help reveal the truth. As Jason observed their expressions, speech and body language, he began to discern who the true mother was.

At first, Jason could not determine which woman was the true mother, as the other child was already dead. His task was to discover which mother's love was the strongest. Although both women showed motherly affection, their sincerity would be revealed when the living child was threatened with death. The woman who was not the true mother knew who the living child was and did not want it to be killed. She refused the sword and stood firm in her honor.

The other woman, however, preferred that the living child be killed rather than give it up. In a compassionate plea, she cried out, *"O my Lord, give the living child to her, but do not see it killed."* The true mother, showing tenderness and compassion for the child of her womb, chose to give up her claim rather than see the child harmed. The other woman, whose child had died, showed no such concern.

The people who witnessed this case were amazed to see how God's wisdom prevailed. This was one of the proofs that God's wisdom is an excellent spirit in all areas of human life. Meekness is a form of wisdom that helps you understand yourself and the weaknesses of human nature. It is slow to anger and knows how to excuse the faults of others as well as its own. Modesty is a badge of wisdom, and heavenly wisdom is more valuable than worldly wealth. Grace is more precious than gold.

Grace is the gift of God's favor, meant for the soul and eternity, while gold is for the body and time. Gold will not stand with you in your final hour, but wisdom and grace will. There is vanity and vexation of spirit in the pursuit of wealth, but joy and satisfaction come from seeking wisdom. *"Great peace have those who love it."*

PRAYER

Dear God, thank You for granting me wisdom to know how to go out and how to come in. Thank You for Your sincere understanding and knowledge, and for the long life in which I will serve You, Lord, in the name of Your Son, Jesus Christ. Father, I stretch my hands to You, for there is no other help I know. Please do not draw Yourself from me, but hold me close to You. Thank You for the hope You offer to those who love You, and thank You for rescuing me from the depths of the edge.

Chapter 18

CHURCH ATTENDANCE

Churches come in all styles and shapes, from secret planning meetings in homes to wide-open gatherings in amphitheaters and worship services packing thousands into a sanctuary while an overflow crowd watches on closed-circuit television. The appearance of a church building may vary, but the church itself is not confined to four walls. The church of Jesus Christ is made up of people, His people, of every race and nation who love Christ and are committed to serving Him.

People don't just decide to attend church without a specific purpose in mind. There are various reasons that may attract individuals to attend church. For example, someone may feel lost and want to be found by someone who can help them. Others may seek love and acceptance, friendship, or someone to listen to their story. Some may come seeking necessities such as shelter, food, clothing, employment, or access to training institutions, hoping these needs will be met. No matter the distance, people are often willing to make the journey to find satisfaction, acceptance and the feeling that others truly care.

The church is often described as a building, a place where believers meet for worship on the designated day of worship. It is a house of prayer, a community hub, a refuge and a spiritual hospital where people seek healing and relief from various afflictions.

A church aims to nurture individuals of all ages and cultures who arrive with wounds: physical, emotional, or spiritual, from past and present struggles. They bring the anxieties of the future and the scars of past terrors, rejection and failure. These individuals are often likened to tender babes in Christ, seeking solace and guidance. Newcomers may view the church as a casualty ward in a hospital, where they expect to be cared for by compassionate "doctors" and "nurses." While some church workers may not be fully mature in their faith, their presence provides hope and encouragement, as they too are in the process of spiritual growth.

Church Attendance

The church provides a warm atmosphere of hope and healing, offering remedies for life's pains, such as prayer, to ease the burdens of those who are hurting. Many people who attend church are not looking for profound answers; they simply want to feel cared for. When this care is evident, hearts open to God's love, and miracles can happen. The Holy Spirit works in such settings, convicting hearts through the preaching of the Word and encouraging individuals to respond and be saved. Every week, people from different backgrounds and cultures gather on Saturdays or Sundays to worship God as their Redeemer.

Whether the worship is formal and liturgical or casual and spontaneous, church services declare the worthiness of God. However, history shows how easily worship can degenerate into empty ritualism when hearts grow hard and God's Word is forgotten. One of the most important benefits of attending church is the opportunity to seek salvation. While salvation doesn't require church attendance, making the effort to enter the house of the Lord often provides spiritual enrichment and encouragement. Welcoming individuals are there to greet visitors, explain things, and answer questions. In church, the gospel of salvation is preached, and through hearing it, many are moved to accept it.

ANITA'S JOURNEY

....

Weeks after returning from "the edge," Anita remained fragile and desperate to find a place of worship. She had never been a regular churchgoer before, but her traumatic experiences made her long for spiritual connection and healing. The pain and terror she had endured left an emotional scar that seemed impossible to overcome. Eventually, Anita found a church near her home and decided to give it a try.

On a Sunday morning, Anita dressed early and made her way to the church. At the entrance, a warm usher greeted her with a handshake and a broad smile, ushering her to a seat. Anita felt an immediate sense of acceptance. The worship, preaching and music deeply moved her, and she decided to return the following week, hoping the church wouldn't feel too strict or limiting on her personal time.

As she reflected on the sermon and songs, Anita remembered how her grandmother used to take her to church. After her grandmother passed away, Anita fell under the care of an aunt who showed little interest in church, leading Anita to drift away from faith and God.

But now, the words of John 15:15 resonated with her: *"You are my friends if you do whatever I command you. No longer do I call you servants, for a servant does not know what his master is doing; but I have called you friends."* Anita thought, "I can't get too friendly with people I hardly know. Perhaps if I keep coming, I will get to know and trust them."

Encouraged to read the Bible given to her as a visitor gift, Anita began to pray daily. This rekindled her spiritual appetite and helped her reflect on her life. Soon, Anita became a regular attendee and was invited to join new convert classes. These sessions helped her grow spiritually, learn more about the Bible, and strengthen her prayer life.

A TESTIMONY OF HEALING

During a church service, Anita shared her testimony, recounting how bad company had led her to "the edge." Her story of regret and redemption deeply moved the congregation. Overwhelmed with emotion, Anita broke down in tears and the church members surrounded her with hugs and words of comfort. This act of love and support lightened her burden and solidified her place in the family of God.

After her public confession of faith, Anita boldly declared her belief in Jesus Christ as her Lord and Savior. Her heartfelt responses to questions about her commitment brought cheers and applause from the congregation, who welcomed her warmly into the body of Christ. Anita's transformation inspired her to reach out to others, inviting them to experience the healing and joy she had found in church.

SHARING THE GOOD NEWS

Anita encouraged her friend Johnny, who had also returned from "the edge," to attend church. Johnny, curious and hopeful, joined her and was touched by the warmth of the church community. He soon decided to invite two more friends, Troy and Melissa, who also attended church and began their journeys of faith.

All five of them participated in baptismal classes, learning foundational Christian principles like repentance, confession, and consecration. The step-by-step classes ensured they were well-prepared for their new lives in Christ. As they shared their testimonies and grew in faith, their stories inspired the church members to reflect on their own roles in evangelism. The congregation realized the power of sharing personal experiences to draw others to Christ and committed to reaching more people for His cause.

A NEW BEGINNING

For Anita, Johnny, Troy, Melissa, and others who joined the church, their transformation marked the beginning of a new chapter. They embraced their new nature as believers and left behind the past, trusting in God's promise to turn darkness into light. Their journey demonstrates that even from "the edge," God's love can rescue and restore, creating a ripple effect that touches countless lives.

REPENTING OF ALL KNOWN WRONGS

....

Repentance is a godly sorrow for wrongdoings, also called sin. Many fail to understand its true nature. Some feel sorrow for their sins out of fear of the consequences they may bring upon themselves. However, true repentance involves both the mind and the heart. It begins with recognizing the wrongness of one's actions and acknowledging that God's standards and will are righteous.

Ignorance or forgetfulness of God's will and standards can act as barriers to repentance. True repentance requires hearing and seeing with understanding. The mind must perceive and grasp the significance of what the eyes see and the ears hear. Yet, more importantly, repentance involves the heart. When the heart is deeply moved, the mind can more easily align itself with God's will, proving to oneself the good, acceptable, and perfect will of God.

Repentance transforms a person's view of themselves, especially when they are in the wrong. It is important to note that a right relationship with God can be lost or diminished due to life's busyness, whether at home, work, or even in church activities. The constant demands of life can drown out the voice of God.

To restore a good relationship with God, take time to reflect on "mirror scriptures" that reveal your true self. These verses can help you see where you stand and guide you back to Him. Remember, Jesus was never too busy to be interrupted; He always had time to listen to the heart's cry.

As a powerful reminder of God's love and willingness to forgive, reflect on John 3:16:

"For God so loved the world that He gave His only begotten Son, that whoever believes in Him should not perish but have everlasting life."

SEPARATION

Christians should live a holy life that reflects the nature of God, who has saved them. This involves separating oneself from actions, influences, or people that may lead to spiritual contamination. By applying biblical principles of separation, believers can avoid anything that contradicts the biblical standard of purity.

(*"For the weapons of our warfare are not carnal but mighty in God for pulling down strongholds."* 2 Corinthians 10:4)

You are called to separate yourself for the sake of others, particularly the weaker brother, by avoiding things that may offend their conscience or hinder their faith. Failure to live as an example of Christ can be a stumbling block for others. A right relationship with the Holy Spirit enables a believer to be both holy and spiritual, aligning their life with God's will.

(*But you are a chosen generation, a royal priesthood, a holy nation, His own special people, that you may proclaim the praises of Him who called you out of darkness into His marvelous light."* 1 Peter 2:9*)*

RECONCILATION AFTER THE EDGE

....

Reconciliation is the act by which God, through Christ's death, eliminated the cause of hostility between

Himself and humanity, enabling a complete and maturing fellowship with Him. The hostility, caused by sin, was removed through the sacrifice on the cross.

Those who have been reconciled to God are also entrusted with the ministry of reconciliation, which is fulfilled when they actively engage in soul-winning and sharing the message of salvation.

(*That is, that God was in Christ reconciling the world to Himself, not imputing their trespasses to them, and has committed to us the word of reconciliation."* 2 Corinthians 5:19)

CONSECRATION

Everyone who loves God and decides to make Him the center of their lives should seek consecration, a life set apart for His purpose and will. Begin each morning by dedicating yourself to God, making this your first work of the day. Spend time in prayer, saying:

"Take me, O Lord, as wholly Yours. I lay all my plans at Your feet. Use me today in Your service. Abide with me, and let all my works be done through You."

As you continue this practice of consecration, you will draw closer to Jesus. The closer you come to Him, the more you will see your own imperfections, for His perfect nature highlights our faults. If you claim to have no sin, you deceive yourself, and the truth is not in you.

Do not be discouraged by this realization. The Spirit of God is working within you. The less you seek to exalt yourself, the more you will appreciate the infinite purity and beauty of your Savior. Never draw back in despair. Instead, bow down and weep at the feet of Jesus, bringing your shortcomings and mistakes to Him. Always remember that Christ is at the right hand of the Father, making intercession for you.

Beloved, trust in God daily, consecrating yourself in prayer, believing more fully, and relying on His strength rather than your own. There is a regenerating power, unseen by human eyes, that creates a new life in the soul, forming a new being in the image of God.

Church Attendance

The work of the Holy Spirit is silent and often imperceptible, but its effects are visible. While you cannot change your heart on your own or bring yourself into harmony with God, the Spirit's work within you transforms you. Fellowship with the brethren also strengthens your faith.

Gather with other believers to share your journey. These gatherings may include vibrant singing, reading of Scripture, and collective prayer. They are invaluable moments of mutual encouragement, building each other up in the faith. Such meetings are uplifting and cannot be replaced by material wealth. They nourish the soul, helping Christians grow spiritually.

As you pray earnestly, the Lord will fill you with awe and gratitude for His marvelous gift of salvation. Prayer empowers you to give Him the praise He deserves and to remain faithful in your love and obedience.

What is fellowship?

FELLOWSHIP ONE WITH ANOTHER

....

Church attendance includes fellowship and commitment with other fellow believers who are united for interaction, and as an aspect of fulfilling the great commandments and building up each other in harmony. Expressing, love and relationship in the church, the body of Christ is extremely essentially important.

Encouraging fellowship with one another and at the same time personally working on attitudes to the glory of God, meeting regularity, having fellowship assisting other believers and growing in worshipping and establishing right foundation, building a right attitude, and be intentionally, reflecting on the things that prevents your growth, and fix it.

People look forward attending church services and participating in activity taking part in various ministry, such as information in community charitable activities,, visiting the sick, and shut ins. some joining choir, playing musical instruments, training on subjects such as, public speaking on how to approach others in street or group settings, clubs for elderly where they can come together and have meaningful discussions on certain days and times in the week. Some may even choose to learn new skills and willingly share among others who are interested. Most people have the privilege to listen to a good sermon reading from the bible on topics regarding life and death, to remind us what the future holds after leaving this world.

GIVING TO A WORTHY CAUSE

There is no better indicator of growth in the new life than in the area of giving. Giving reflects the attitude of the heart, it should be done cheerfully, for cheerful giving often leads to generosity. The importance of giving is not determined by how much is given, but by the spirit in which it is offered and how much is left behind. All the money in the world belongs to God; therefore, our gifts to Him do not make Him any richer. Instead, they enrich us spiritually, reminding us that everything we have comes from Him and that we give because we love Him.

If you are a strong and capable individual, no one will penalize you for giving towards the upkeep of the church where you and your family worship. However, it is a long-term benefit to give something from the resources God has provided you. Failing to willingly offer the money God has entrusted to you is a serious matter.

When someone neglects to honor God with their finances, they rob Him, not because it impoverishes God, but because it denies the means He has ordained for supporting His work and ministries. For those who faithfully honor God with their resources, He promises abundant blessings.

"Bring the whole tithe into the storehouse, that there may be food in my house. Test me in this," says the Lord Almighty, "and see if I will not throw open the floodgates of heaven and pour out so much blessing that there will not be room enough to store it." (Malachi 3:10)

PRAYER

....

Dear God, our Father how much I adore and praise your holy name. Thank you for the power of your name and the access you have given to use your wonderful and gracious name. Thank you for purchasing the church of Jesus Christ and fully paid for by the His blood shed on the cross of Calvary. Lest

Church Attendance

I forget what you bore for the sins of the entire human race, please remind me again. I kindly ask these mercies in the name of your beloved Son Jesus Christ.

BOUNCING BACK FROM THE EDGE

Chapter 12

ABIDING ON THE STRAIGHT AND NARROW

To abide means to remain, dwell, endure, or continue in a permanent state. Abiding on the straight and narrow can be likened to abiding in Jesus, who is the way, the truth, and the life. It means continually receiving and believing in the truth that Jesus is everything you need. The secret to abiding on the straight and narrow path lies in obeying and keeping God's commands. The only safe way to remain on this path is through consistent reliance on and adherence to the Word of God. Staying on the straight and narrow is not a casual commitment but an ongoing, intentional choice to abide.

True abiding means constant faithfulness, it is not about hopping on when it's convenient or hopping off when it's not. It requires a stable, permanent commitment in all circumstances. Abiding in Christ empowers you to walk confidently on the straight and narrow. Those who abide in Christ will never be abandoned by Him. As Jesus said, *"If My words abide in you, ask whatever you will, and it shall be done for you."*

As a traveler on the road of life, you will always need a guide. When you abide in Christ, He will never fail to lead or sustain you. Just as a tree planted in good soil produces abundant, nourishing fruit, those who abide in Christ bear spiritual fruit that benefits others. A tree with strong roots does not wither or lose its branches, and so it is with those who abide in Him.

The first story in this book illustrates this truth. It tells of a boy named Raymond, his brother Marlon and their father. Raymond, the central figure, left his father's house and made a mess of his life. He experienced hardship and despair, living on the edge, so close to ruin, symbolized by his time near the pigpen. Yet, through the fervent prayers of his father, Raymond survived and ultimately returned home.

Raymond often reflected on his journey, recalling how he left his father's house full but returned empty. His incredible story, shared with those he encountered, became a powerful testimony. Through his experiences, others learned valuable lessons, taking heed of his mistakes to avoid finding themselves on the edge.

Raymond, along with many others who have victoriously bounced back from the edge, made the conscious decision to abide in Jesus and His Word. Remaining in Him while continuing on the straight and narrow path is essential; pursuing any other course without taking deliberate action can lead to serious and even fatal consequences. Everyone who reports a comeback in this book should take heed of these suggestions on how to abide on the straight and narrow road.

This path, called life, is unique. It features many roads that lead to or diverge from it, some are narrow, while others are wide. On the wide path, you will find crowds of busy people moving to and fro with ease. However, the narrow path is different. It's more challenging, less traveled, and requires perseverance. Walking on this path demands a strong desire to abide, to remain steadfast and to adhere to the principles clearly marked by the road signs along the way. You must be vigilant, constantly reading and following any changes or warnings ahead.

For those returning from the edge, it's crucial to listen carefully to the positive experiences of others who have also bounced back, no matter what brought them to the brink. These testimonies serve as encouragement, inspiring others to aim for the narrow path and rebuild their lives according to God's Word. God desires humanity to exercise its reasoning powers, and studying the Bible can strengthen and elevate the mind like no other endeavor. While some aspects of Scripture may seem difficult or obscure, God will make them plain and simple to those who sincerely seek understanding.

However, reading the Bible without reverence or prayer, without fixing one's thoughts and affections on God, can result in little to no benefit, and in some cases, may even cause harm. Skepticism can take root when the Word of God is approached with a casual or irreverent attitude. To stay on the narrow path, it is vital to remain in God's Word consistently. Let it serve as a covering for your mind, guarding against confusion and distractions. Always remember to use the Word of God as your road map and constant guide.

Those who are truly seeking communion with God are often found in prayer meetings, faithfully fulfilling their duties and earnestly striving to reap the spiritual benefits available to them. They take every opportunity to position themselves where they can receive the light of heaven. To abide on the straight and narrow path, travelers must be observant of the actions and distractions around them, as well as the vile and wicked intentions that might arise. This road is not for the uncommitted or the foolish; it is reserved for ambitious overcomers and those with humble spirits.

The straight and narrow road does not attract many, even though its light shines brightly in all seasons. Few are willing to travel this path because it requires courage, discipline, stability and tenacity. The narrow road is not without challenges; it has its bends, and ongoing "road work" represents the process of growth and reconstruction that strengthens and sustains those on it. At times, the repairs and adjustments can be confusing or distracting, but they are necessary to make the road enduring.

On this road, there is no option for a U-turn due to its inherent dangers. Once you enter, you are expected to move forward steadily until the journey's end. Many who have bounced back from the edge of despair find themselves numbered among those traveling this road. They often refer to it as the *Victory Road*, a place of reflection and triumph.

Travelers share a joyful atmosphere, encouraging one another by recounting their journey: stories of redemption that range from deeply moving to life-transforming. These people come from all walks of life, representing various cultures, ethnicities, gender and ages. Hearing each individual's initial reaction to their *"return home"* is inspiring, filled with excitement, joy, and tears of gladness for achieving long-awaited promises. Many may even sing songs of victory.

Those who abide constantly on the straight and narrow path discover peace, quietness, and confidence in their journey. They understand that trusting in the Lord brings justification and righteousness before God. Such travelers enjoy access to God's treasure house of blessings and are welcomed into His family. True righteousness and personal fulfillment come not from worldly achievements, such as stability at home, influential friends, or a six-figure income, but from abiding in God's presence and promises.

The treasure of God's people lies in the fear of the Lord and a reverent obedience to Him. This relationship, rooted in trust and faith in Christ as Savior, is vital and life-changing. Knowledge of God's truth is also essential, but mere knowledge without action is meaningless. For example, someone who learns the location of a buried treasure but does nothing to claim it remains as impoverished as before.

Acting upon the knowledge of God's Word leads to spiritual wealth and fulfillment, which far surpasses anything the world can offer.

Embarking on the journey of abiding on the straight and narrow path calls for preparation, reflection, and discipline. Taking the time to assess your spiritual readiness beforehand can be incredibly beneficial. Here are some important steps to help you stay grounded and focused on this path:

CULTIVATE A DESIRE FOR SPIRITUAL GROWTH

Begin by asking God to open your spiritual eyes, enabling you to see the truth of His Word and His will for your life. For those who struggle with spiritual insight, pray for clarity and perception. Ask for the opening of your spiritual ears, so you can hear His voice and discern His guidance more clearly.

EMBRACE GOD'S RESTORATIVE POWER

Trust in God's ability to restore and empower. He strengthens those who feel spiritually crippled, enabling them to do His work. To those who feel mute, He provides the ability to express themselves and share His truth, filling their hearts with songs of praise. Abiding in His presence brings joy, renewal, and a deep sense of peace as you draw close to a loving and gracious Father who invites all to come to Him for rest.

DEVELOP STABILITY THROUGH GOD'S WORD

God understands that you cannot remain steadfast on your own. Life's challenges can feel overwhelming, but He offers stability and strength through His Word. His guidance prevents you from being tossed about like a ship in a stormy sea or carried away like clouds by winds of false doctrines. The best method you can take to fortify against such is to study the word of God and pray for illumination and grace.

FORTIFY YOURSELF WITH STUDY AND PRAYER

To remain firm, you must commit to studying the Word of God and seeking Him through prayer. Ask for illumination and grace to understand His truth and apply it in your daily life. This practice will build resilience, clarity, and confidence as you walk the straight and narrow path.

By following these steps and depending on God's presence and power, you can remain on the straight and narrow path with joy and assurance. He will provide the strength, stability, and wisdom needed for the journey, ensuring you are firmly rooted in His truth and grace.

PRAYER

Father, thank You so much for keeping us steadfast on the straight and narrow way. Your Word assures us that You will keep what we have committed to You. With Your guidance and leading, I will not return to the edge, no matter how rough the way, no matter how often I pause to pray. My heart is set on reaching that eternal city on the evergreen shore.

Truly, Father, You are gracious in mercy and full of compassion. Your faithfulness toward us is beyond comprehension. Thank You for considering us, even amidst our struggles and challenges.

You were always there, ever-present and unfailing. For this, we are eternally grateful. Amen.

ACKNOWLEDGEMENTS

I wish to extend my heartfelt thanks to all my encouragers and readers of my previous books. Your unwavering support means the world to me. Grace and peace be to you all from God, our Father,
and the Lord Jesus Christ.

- Bishop Louie McLeod -
New Testament Church of God, Lee District – A steadfast supporter.

- Rev. Pastor Richard Young -
Charlton New Testament Church of God – Always uplifting me in prayer and providing continual support.

- Rev. Bishop D Henry -
An excellent educator who generously made time for meaningful discussions and important questions that enriched this manuscript.

- Mrs. Carolyn & Mr. Lyn van Anderson -
Counselor and supervisor in the dental industry – Thank you for your unwavering encouragement during pivotal moments.

PREVIOUS BOOKS

1. A GUIDE TO EFFECTIVE PRAYER - *Written and published 2012*

2. AFTER THE HONEYMOON - *Written and published 2013*

3. GOD IS ALWAYS RIGHT - *Written and published 2020*

4. THE EFFECTIVENESS OF THE NAMES OF GOD - *Written and published 2022*

5. THE EDGE - *Written and published 2022*

6. ATTITUDES FOR FRUITFUL CHRISTIAN LIVING - *Written and published 2023*

www.ingramcontent.com/pod-product-compliance
Lightning Source LLC
Chambersburg PA
CBHW072149070526
44585CB00015B/1059